Pub Walks in the Yorkshire Dales

Clive Price

Published by Sigma Leisure – an imprint of
Sigma Press, 1 South Oak Lane, Wilmslow, Cheshire SK9 6AR, England.

Whilst every effort has been made to ensure that the information given in this book is correct, neither the publisher nor the author accept any responsibility for any inaccuracy.

British Library Cataloguing in Publication Data
A CIP record for this book is available from the British Library.

ISBN: 1-85058-299-8

Typesetting and Design by: Sigma Press, Wilmslow, Cheshire.
For the technically-minded: the original typescript was scanned electronically into a form that could be read by Microsoft Word version 5.5 on an IBM PC-compatible. The files were then checked, with some human intervention, with the Grammatik 5 style and grammar checking software. The final design was completed with DESKpress desktop publishing software, which also generated the contents pages.

Cover photograph: The New Inn, Clapham – a 200 year old former coaching inn, set in a picturesque village in the heart of the Yorkshire Dales.

Printed by: Manchester Free Press

PREFACE

My first visit to the Yorkshire Dales was made at the age of 13 when I spent a week's holiday in Beamsley. During those seven days I walked the path along the Wharfe between Bolton Bridge and Burnsall and climbed over Barden Fell to Simon's Seat and Lord's Seat.

From those vantage points a desire was born to explore the distant horzons and beyond. Subsequently that ambition was fulfilled but even now I never tire of gazing at the views offered by the high points of the Dales.

Initially, my tender age prescribed any intimate knowledge of the hostelries of the region. Maturity remedied that defect. Therefore I was thrilled when invited to compile this selection of 30 walks. I was able to re-visit familiar places but, even more exciting was the opportunity to investigate some of the hidden corners of the Dales with which even I was unfamiliar. I hope this volume will entice you to follow in my footsteps and to keep my seat warm for me in the snug.

There are several people I must thank for their help and assistance in making this book possible.

Graham Beech of Sigma Press for his patience and advice. Colin Speakman for his suggestions, Steve Hounsham and other members of the staff of the Yorkshire Dales National Park,and members of the staff of Central Reference Library, Manchester, and of Richmond Library.

It would be discourteous of me if I failed to offer my thanks to all the landlords and landladies who have made me so welcome in their hostelries.

Finally I must thank all the members of my family for coping so well when I have been away from home. It is to them that I dedicate this book.

Clive Price

CONTENTS

CONTENTS

INTRODUCTION

Choosing the Walks

There are thousands of walks in the Yorkshire Dales. To single out 30 was a difficult, almost impossible task.

The notion of basing each on a pub went some considerable distance towards alleviating the problem but, with more than 100 hostelries in the region, did not eradicate it completely. Further limitations of choice followed from a decision not to encourage drinking and driving. Only pubs accessible by public transport were regarded as eligible. One result was that many fine pubs and equally fine walks had to be omitted.

Nidderdale, for example, suffered in this respect because it enjoys neither bus nor train service beyond Pateley Bridge. It fell victim, too, to another criterion stipulating that all the walks had to be within the confines of the National Park, although one or two do cross the boundary. When the National Park was established Nidderdale was excluded because Bradford Corporation, which then owned a string of reservoirs in the valley, pressurised the government of the day into drawing the Park's borders around the boundaries of its holdings.

Even when all these restrictions had been laid down, the choice of walks remained wide. In the last analysis the final 30 were the outcome of personal inclination but aimed at providing as wide a geographical and topographical spread as possible. While it was felt that some popular locations should be included, other walks were designed to encourage the rambler to explore new areas of equal beauty within the National Park.

Erosion in the countryside has become a major problem, the result of too many boots following in the wake of others. The National Park Authority is currently devoting considerable energy and not a little cash to fighting this, especially in the area surrounding the Three Peaks of Ingleborough, Whernside and Pen-y-ghent. That posed another difficulty. Should more people be encouraged to visit these summits? On the other hand was it realistic to compile a selection of walks in the Dales without including them? Finally, after deep and prolonged thought, a compromise was reached. Only one peak would be chosen. That was Ingleborough because it lends itself better than either of the other two to devising route alternatives.

So, by one means or another, the required 30 pubs and routes were finally selected. Not only do the walks pass through some magnificent scenery but most have other points of interest as well, whether it be architectural, historical or botanical.

The Pubs

The pubs featured in this selection of walks come in all shapes and sizes. Some are small with stone-flagged floors, tiny bars, and unplastered stone walls. Others have been modernised. Many are plain country establishments while others provide en-suite accommodation and serve full-scale meals in first-class restaurants.

Most are old, one possibly dating back to the twelfth or thirteenth century. Others were established during the heyday of the coaching era when several roads through the Dales were turnpiked.

There are pubs with Hiker's Bars where they expect mud on the floor and there are pubs where they politely invite you to remove your dirty footwear before entering. No matter into which of these two categories they fall, all of them will offer a genuinely warm welcome. In winter this hospitality is typified by the roaring log fires.

Most, if not all nowadays, provide bar meals ranging from the simple ham sandwich to a more substantial dish. These provide as important a part of the landlord's income as do the drinks he serves. Throughout the Dales there is a uniformly high standard of cuisine linked with helpings which can only be described as "more than large".

In almost all cases the ales mentioned are hand-drawn on pump. In the more northerly dales there is a tendency for most houses to offer Theakston's Ales. Although this brewery is no longer independent the quality of the various brews remains high. Dent Bitter, with its companion, Ram's Bottom, is slowly spreading and one enterprising pub in Swaledale serves Conciliation Ale from the new Butterknowle brewery in neighbouring Teesdale. Further south, the big breweries make their presence felt but even here the smaller ones such as Timothy Taylor's are still well represented.

Many of the pubs in the Dales are Free Houses with many licensees offering their customers special guest beers which are changed at frequent intervals. There is a practice, too, of offering a wider range of beers during the summer months when trade is brisker. The information contained in this book is correct at the time of writing but it is a sad fact of life that some of the pubs in these remote villages tend to change hands rather more often than in some areas. With greater flexibility allowed these days it is possible that opening times may change from time to time. Especially in high summer and a week-ends, some landlords may stay open all day.

Finally, one other quality common to them all is that they are all surrounded by beautiful countryside.

The Village Green, Carperby

The Yorkshire Dales

Stand on the platform of Ribblehead Station waiting for the train as dusk falls during the mid-afternoon of a gloomy, late November day and gaze out over Batty Moss towards Whernside, or towards Cam End over Gearstones. In such circumstances it is impossible to believe that most of the Yorkshire Dales was once part of a tropical sea.

Yet, more than 300 million years ago that was the case. Those seas were swarming with fish and animals which, when they died, left their shells to form the limestone that is now the hallmark of the Dales. Muds and other debris carried by rivers feeding that sea laid down other rock such as sandstone and gritstone and shales on top of the limestone to form the layered formations now known as the Yoredale series. These are evident near the summits of the Three Peaks and in many of the Dales.

In due course the Ice Age arrived, covering the landscape with enromous glaciers which carved out many of the valleys. As they retreated they left deposits of glacial deposits or morraine, two of which acted as dam walls for the two natural lakes of the region, Semerwater and Malham Tarn.

Weathering by wind, rain and frost has formed the surface layers, especially on the limestone pavements which are such a feature of the area. However, the Dales has some vast areas of peat moorland, especially above Ribblehead, Kettlewell, Coverdale and on the northern side of Swaledale. These high moorlands form the water-sheds for the major rivers. This is evident from the different directions taken by the rivers. The Swale and Ure flow eastwards to form the Yorkshire Ouse where they are joined by the Wharfe and Aire which, initially, flow southwards.

The Rawthey and Dee head towards the west to join the Lune on its way to the Irish Sea while the Ribble takes a southerly direction before turning to the west on entering Lancashire. Most of the major rivers are fed by minor ones such as the Cover, the Bain and Arkle Beck. The rushing, babbling waters of these rivers, and the myriad of streams which flow from the moors and limestone edges, have created scores of waterfalls, or 'forces' as they are often known, which attract increasing numbers of visitors each year. Water, too, has been mainly responsible for the scores of caves, potholes and sink holes which pepper the dales, a mecca for the keen caver.

Human history has done much to fashion the landscape. Evidence of Stone Age settlement has been unearthed at Yockenthwaite in Upper Wharfedale and at Castle Dykes near Aysgarth. The Romans exploited the lead deposits, to safeguard which they built a fort a little to the east of the present village of Bainbridge. Their road over Cam End into Ribblesdale and on to Ingleton and Lancaster is now used by ramblers.

The Norse settlers bequeathed the Dales with a rich heritage of place-names ranging from Keld and Muker to Thwaite and Arkengarthdale. They also introduced the Norwegian name "Seter" into the English language through their practice of moving their cattle to the upper or higher pastures for summer grazing. This name is perpetuated in Countersett, Marsett and Appersett in Wensleydale. The tradition of the remote and isolated field barn, so much a part of the Dales landscape, also derives from this practice.

Field barns, near Hawes

The Normans brought their castles to Middleham and Richmond and they converted large areas into hunting forests such as Langstrothdale Chase and Middleham Moor, now used for training racehorses.

In the Norman era the great abbeys of Bolton, Fountains and Jervaulx were built. The monks acquired extensive estates in the Dales which they converted into enormous ranges for their flocks of sheep. In the more remote areas they established granges for the management of their lands. To connect these with the mother houses they developed a network of routes which have continued through to the present day as bridleways. Mastiles Lane, near Malham, is one of the finest examples. Other lanes are the result of the Scottish and Northern England drovers guiding herds of cattle and sheep to the markets and fairs that were held both in the Dales and beyond.

Economic activity was not confined to farming. Many of the Dales and the surrounding hillsides are littered with the scars of lead mining. The flues, hushes, smelting houses and spoil heaps now blend into the landscape to add a further point of interest for the walker. Coal, too, was mined on the moors surrounding Tan Hill and in Ingleton. These industries also created tracks across a wide area. Some were later turnpiked, as the current road through Arkengarthdale, but others survived simply as bridleways and now form a vital part of the footpath network.

As these traditional industries declined, the prosperity of many villages and small towns was maintained by the development of tourism. Every summer thousands of people flock into the Dales to visit such beauty spots as the Aysgarth Falls and Hardraw Force. Others are attracted to such historical remains as Bolton Abbey or Middleham Castle. Some come simply to escape the urban environment in which they live and work. Almost every village has its pub, cafe or tea room. The new licensing laws mean that many pubs now choose to remain open all day in the summer or at busy week-ends.

In 1953 the Yorkshire Dales National Park was established to conserve this unique landscape. It is responsible for maintaining all the footpaths within its boundaries and for protecting the landscape which it does through its planning controls. Another duty is to help the visitor to enjoy quiet relaxation while, at the same time, allowing the farmer to get on with his work. This is often a fine balancing act which it carries out through its warden service. The National Park has also built several information centres and car parks to cater for the visitor.

Yorkshire Dales National Park Information Centre, Malham

Public Transport

To encourage greater use of public transport and to discourage driving and drinking, details of public transport have been included for each individual walk. These were correct at the time of writing but since de-regulation changes to services have become more frequent. Therefore it is advisable to check before setting out.

Many of the Dales are served by regular scheduled services. Other areas depend on buses which run only occasionally or even on certain days of the week. Some services, especially on Saturdays and Sundays, are specially subsidised by the Yorkshire Dales National Park. These are known as "Dalesbuses" and usually start from towns outside the park boundaries.

The prolonged struggle to keep the Settle – Carlisle railway line open has finally been won, thereby maintaining a service which not only caters for the local inhabitants but also for the walker. This does not operate on winter Sundays but is a 7-days a week service during the summer. On specified Sundays during the summer trains from Stockport, Manchester, Blackpool and Preston are operated along the line.

Intending visitors should obtain a copy of "Dales Connections". This guide is published by Elmtree Publications with support from the Yorkshire Dales National Park. It is available free from all National Park Information Centres or direct from the National Park Offices in Grassington. A list of operators with their telephone numbers is given below:

British Rail
Leeds 448133; Skipton 792543; Settle 823536; Carlisle 44711.

Bus companies
Cumberland Motor Services: Kendal 733221
Harrogate and District: Harrogate 566061
Keighley and District: Keighley 603284
Keighley and District: Skipton 795331
Lakeland Coaches: Blackburn 86646
Lancaster City Transport: Lancaster 424555
Mountain Goat: Windermere 5161
Pennine Motors: Skipton 749215
Ribble Motor Services: Lancaster 64228
Skipton Busways: Settle 822449
United Bus Company: Darlington 468771
Whaites Coaches: Settle 823235
J. Woof: Sedbergh 20414.

National Park Centres
Aysgarth Falls: Wensleydale 663424
Clapham: Clapham 419
Grassington: Grassington 752748
Hawes: Wensleydale 667450
Malham: Airton 363
Sedbergh: Sedbergh 201125.

There are, also, several National Park information points with a limited number of maps and leaflets located in cafes and post offices throughout the Park.

Practical Notes

Although many of these walks involve steep climbs, and equally steep descents, none of them lead the walker over razor-sharp ridges where one slip may have serious consequences. Any person of average fitness should be capable of completing them.

However, there is always the chance of cutting a finger on barbed wire or slipping on wet rock. So, it is advisable to carry a small first-aid kit. These may be purchased from outdoor shops or you may prefer to assemble your own.

Another useful piece of equipment is a whistle with which to summon help in case of emergencies. On some of the longer walks over higher ground a bivvy bag may be useful for affording warmth to anyone waiting for help to arrive.

Maps

The maps in this guide are general in nature. The route descriptions should be used in conjunction with the appropriate 1:25000 Ordnance Survey map. Details of the appropriate ones are given with each walk.

Boots

A good pair of walking boots is essential. Many of the routes cross rough and stoney ground which will ruin ordinary shoes. Even the low level paths across fields and by riversides are usually muddy. Neither wellingtons nor trainers are recommended because they are designed for other purposes. Today there are many lightweight designs on the market which will prove adequate for any of these walks.

To provide extra comfort inside the walking boots, walking socks are advised. They are also warmer.

Clothing

Bearing in mind the vagaries of the British weather it is essential that rainwear should be carried at all times. Preferably this should include a cagoule, with hood, and overtrousers.

Even when the weather is hot and sunny in the valleys the temperatures on the fell tops will be a few degrees lower. Therefore, always carry a spare pullover.

In early Spring, late Autumn and Winter, thicker layers of clothing will be required as well as an anorak which will give adequate protection against winds and low temperatures.

Location Map

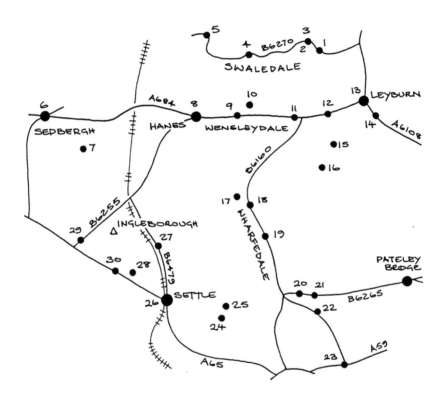

1. FREMINGTON EDGE

A varied walk, starting with an easy stroll through the valley of the Swale to a medieval priory but followed by a stiff climb onto one of the most outstanding limestone escarpments in the Yorkshire Dales National Park.

Route: Grinton Bridge – Marrick Priory – Marrick – Fremington Edge – White House – Fremington – Grinton Bridge.

Distance: $7^1/_2$ miles

Start: Grinton Bridge Hotel, on the B6270. Map reference 046985.

Map: Ordnance Survey Outdoor Leisure Map number 30, "Yorkshire Dales, Northern and Central Areas".

Public transport: Bus service number 30, Richmond – Gunnerside. Daily except Sundays. United Bus Company.

Car: Grinton Bridge is on the B6270 Richmond – Muker road through Swaledale. Parking, for patrons only, at the Bridge Hotel.

THE BRIDGE HOTEL, GRINTON-IN-SWALEDALE

Yvonne Jackson is the second longest-serving licensee in Swaledale but her enthusiasm is as fresh as ever. The Bridge Hotel, however, enjoys a much longer history. Standing by one of the most important crossing points of the River Swale, it dates mainly from the seventeenth century although one section, the cottage-end, is reputed to be as old as the medieval parish church across the road.

In its time, it has served as a coaching inn and today is extremely popular with Coast-to-Coast walkers who call in either to slake their thirst or to enjoy one of its excellent bar meals or even to take advantage of its overnight accommodation. It has a cosy bar offering Theakston's Bitter and Old Peculier alongside John Smith's Magnet and Bitter, all the ales being cask conditioned.

Opening Times: Monday to Saturday, 11.00 to 15.00 and 18.00 to 23.00; Sunday, 12.00 to 15.00 and 19.00 to 22.30.

The Bridge Hotel, Grinton

GRINTON BRIDGE

The bridge, from which the hotel takes its name, was designed by the celebrated York architect, John Carr. It was constructed in 1797 but, according to John Leland, writing in the 1540s, there was already "a fair bridge" on the same site.

ST. ANDREW'S CHURCH

From the Norman Conquest until the reign of Elizabeth I, when a new church was built at Muker higher up the valley, St.Andrew's, Grinton, served the entire length of Swaledale. Because it possessed the only consecrated ground, the dead were carried on biers from as far afield as Keld and Thwaite. The route followed, sections of which are still used by ramblers, became recognised as the "Corpse Road".

Fragments of the Norman foundation of St.Andrews still survive but the main portions of the church date from the years between the thirteenth and fifteenth centuries. One notable feature is the "Lepers'

Squint", a hole which allowed the afflicted to observe the service while remaining isolated from the other worshippers.

MARRICK PRIORY

Situated just behind Marrick Priory Farm, the former priory is now used partly as a parish church and partly as an outdoor education centre. It was a twelfth century establishment of Benedictine nuns.

STEPS WOOD

Steps Wood derives its name from the flagged steps, allegedly 365 of them, which link the Priory with the nearby village of Marrick. They have stood the test of time and should provide a useful lesson for anyone engaged in the repair of badly eroded footpaths in the countryside.

They were used by the villagers for attending services in the priory which, unusually, escaped serious destruction during the Dissolution of the Monasteries.

The artist Turner paid a visit to Marrick during his wanderings through the Dales and is reputed to have forded the River Swale at this point.

THE WALK

From the hotel take the B6270 in the direction of Reeth. Once over the bridge turn right onto the path which has the Swale on the right and a wall on the left.

After the sixth stile there is a short climb of 25 yards to a seventh which affords access to a metalled lane at Ewelop Hill, turn right along this lane to reach Marrick Priory after half a mile. Just beyond the Priory Farm, and about ten yards after a cattle grid, turn through a small gate on the left which carries the initials of the Coast-to-Coast walk. Climb the broad green path diagonally right to another small gate after which the surface becomes flagged as it continues rising steeply through Steps Wood.

The path leaves the wood through a small gate adorned with the picture of a bull and climbs to the left of a stone wall. After passing through a five-barred gate, it runs between two stone barns, one

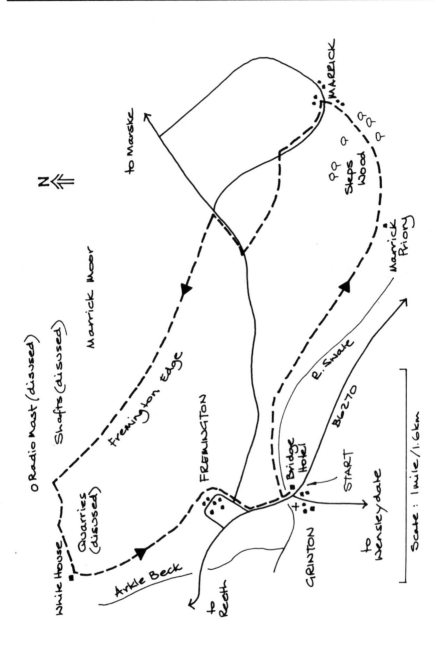

large, the other small, and two further gates. Beyond the second is a tiny Wesleyan Chapel on the left bearing the date 1878

From that point onwards, the path acquires a rough surface as it enters Marrick, a small hamlet of scattered houses. On arriving at the road by a telephone kiosk turn left to pass the Manor House on the right and another called "The White Horse". According to the present owner this was formerly a pub but is now a private residence. Parts of it date back at least to the seventeenth century.

Stay with the minor road through the village but, 300 yards beyond the last farm, turn left through a small gate alongside a footpath sign. Stay to the left of the wall but, ten yards before a five-barred gate, turn right through another small gate and then immediately left, thereby maintaining direction. There is now a wall to the left.

Pass beneath some overhead power lines, negotiate yet another small gate followed by a stile and a five-barred gate to reach the Reeth to Marske road.

Turn right along this for 300 yards. By the junction with another unclassified road, also leading to Marrick, turn left through the gate which has a "NO TIPPING" sign adjacent.

The broad, clear path climbs by some small disused quarries, initially with a wall on the right. However, after a gated stile the wall transfers to the left. This is the south-eastern terminus of Fremington Edge.

Although in parts littered with spoil heaps resulting from the extensive quarrying for chert, it offers some very wide-ranging views as it runs high above Swaledale and Arkengarthdale. The vast expanse of Marrick Moor, clothed in heather, rolls away to the right and the grouse maintain their repeated calls. August is obviously a prime month for enjoying this part of the walk.

Eventually the gradient eases to offer one and a half miles of splendid walking, uninterrupted by either gates or stiles. Shortly after passing a cairn and a cluster of spoil heaps, the path heads to a very conspicuous ladder stile with the rusting skeleton of an abandoned radio mast on the far side of the wall.

Do not use the ladder stile. Instead, turn left over an almost obscure stile set into the wall to follow a vague path with a wall and the radio mast just to the right.

After a short distance the path widens into a rough track which corkscrews steeply down through the abandoned quarry workings until it reaches a bridleway near the White House.

Turn right along this to continue the descent. At a T-junction by the White House, turn left along another wide track, soon passing the entrance to High Bank House to arrive in the hamlet of High Fremington.

At the first junction turn right and, after a few yards, fork left to walk on the outside of a castellated boundary wall to a minor road. Turn right along this for ten yards to meet the B6270. Turn left to recross John Carr's bridge and to regain the hotel in Grinton after a quarter of a mile.

2. REETH

An outward route along the edge of heather-covered moorland is balanced by a return on riverside paths after visiting some of the finest remains of the lead mining industry in Swaledale.

Route: Reeth – Thirns – Surrender Bridge – Old Gang Beck – Healaugh-Reeth.

Distance: 8 miles.

Start: Black Bull Hotel, Reeth, Swaledale. Map reference 037993.

Map: Ordnance Survey Outdoor Leisure Map number 30, "Yorkshire Dales, Northern and Central Areas".

Public transport: Bus service number 30, Richmond – Gunnerside – Keld. Daily except Sundays. United Bus Company.

Dalesbus service number 803, Leeds – Harrogate – Reeth – Hawes. Summer Sundays and Bank Holidays only. Harrogate and District Bus Company.

Car: Reeth is on the B6270 Richmond-Keld road through Swaledale. There is parking around the village green (honesty box).

THE BLACK BULL, REETH

The Black Bull is one of several old coaching inns standing on High Row and facing onto the village green in Reeth. The building itself dates from the seventeenth century. Whenever the weather warrants it, there is a blazing open fire at each end of the L-shaped bar which has settle seats half-way round, along with tables and chairs.

Customers have a choice from Theakston's Bitter, XB, Old Peculier, all drawn from the wood, or Tetley's Bitter which is cask conditioned. If none of these appeal there is also a choice between John Smith's Magnet and Bitter. The Black Bull serves a wide range of bar meals and also has some very pleasant overnight accommodation.

Opening Times: Summer: Monday to Saturday, 11.00 to 23.00; Sunday, 12.00 to 15.00 and 19.00 to 22.30; Winter: Mondays to Saturday, 11.30 to 15.00 and 18.00 to 23.00.

REETH

The village of Reeth occupies a commanding position at the confluence of Arkle Beck with the River Swale, making it an important communication centre. Following the grant of a market charter in 1695 it flourished for almost two centuries, its prosperity based mainly on the twin industries of sheep farming and lead.

It benefitted further from the early turnpiking of the road from Tan Hill, through Arkengarthdale, mainly for the transport of coal. This acted as a spur for the building of several coaching inns which still stand around the village green.

Today the picture had changed. The population has plummetted from an all-time peak of 1,300 to about 300. Although the autumn sheep sales still play an important role in the local economy the village relies heavily on tourism. At the low end of the sloping green the Swaledale Folk Museum is housed in a former Methodist schoolroom. Its wide range of exhibits illustrate the different facets of Swaledale life through the centuries.

LEAD MINING

Surrender Lead Smelting Mill is a reminder of the days when lead mining was the most important industry in this part of Swaledale. The remains are scheduled as an Ancient Monument and conserved by the Yorkshire Dales National Park. The mill is one of several in the vicinity, the more famous Old Gang Mill being a short distance away on the far side of the road.

Lead mining is known to have taken place on these remote moorlands in Roman times but the industry reached its peak during the eighteenth and nineteenth centuries. Many mines were owned by Lord Wharton and in 1770 there were at least four smelt mills operating along the course of Mill Beck or Old Gang Beck as it is variously known.

THE WALK

From the Black Bull join the main road through Reeth, the B6270, as it heads up Swaledale towards Keld passing, on the right, the finest of village bakeries.

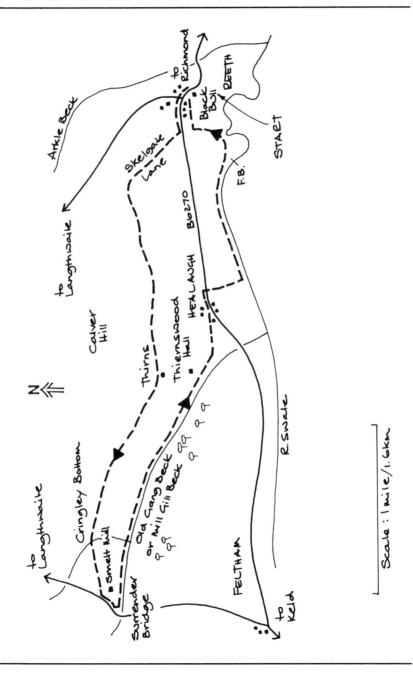

After 300 yards make a right turn into Skelgate, a walled lane which, from the top of the first rise, offers excellent views Of Fremington Edge.

By a facing gate swing left, still between walls but, where two gates flank the route, turn right to climb well above Riddings Farm.

A five-barred wooden gate signals the end of the lane. Beyond this maintain direction along a grassy path to the right of a stone wall. Where this ends aim for a cairn, at the same time keeping to the edge of the moors of Black Hill until meeting another wall on the left.

Stay alongside this wall for some considerable distance, enjoying the views, especially towards Upper Swaledale where one range of moorlands is succeeded by another.

A short distance beyond the termination of the wall and by a black corrugated hut, there is a Y-junction. Fork left to cross open country before descending through an abandoned quarry on a broad track to pass in front of "Moorcock" house to arrive at Thirns Farm.

At the junction of paths there turn right and, after 100 yards and at a second Y-junction, take the path off to the right as it climbs back onto the heather-covered flanks of Calver Hill, soon passing about 50 yards to the left of a large walled enclosure.

By a derelict barn the track converts into a wide grassy path immediately to the right of a wall. Cringley Hill is now visible to the right.

On reaching a small gate set into a facing wall there is a sharp, short drop into Cringley Bottom, an idyllic green oasis cradled by heather moors. It is a place to pause, to absorb and to enjoy. It makes the perfect location for a coffee break or even for lunch, depending on time of day.

Cross the narrow stream, climb the path up the opposite bank and continue forward guided by the small cairns until arriving at the Feetham to Langthwaite road made famous by the television series, "All Creatures Great and Small" which was often filmed in this area.

The narrow, unfenced road is an ancient packhorse and drovers' route between Bowes and Askrigg. Turn left along it but, 20 yards before Surrender Bridge, take the broad track on the left which leads almost at once to the ruins of Surrender lead smelting mill.

Surrender Smelt Mill

The track skirts to the right of the conserved mill buildings before heading-off over the brow of a hill and along an embankment above Old Gang Beck. Soon it corkscrews down to re-cross Cringley Beck. From the far bank it climbs to a gated stile in a facing wall. Beyond this, cross a series of pastures on a well-defined path, using the stiles as an added guide.

On coming face-to-face with a wall without a stile, swing right through a patch of bracken and follow the narrow path on the right-hand side of a wall. The beck is below.

After the next small gate the ruins of Low Cringley Farm may be seen a little distance away to the left. The path again resumes its course across a series of fields, using either stiles or wall gaps before reaching a gateway with Nova Scotia Farm up to the left.

There, at a Y-junction, fork right over two further fields before entering a wood. On leaving this by a stile, stay along the path as it twists its way down a meadow to a squeezer stile.

Beyond, turn right along another broad track. This goes through more woodland and, subsequently, to the right of Thiernswood Hall.

Ten yards after a stone barn, turn left through a stile. Cross the field diagonally to a gated stile located, three quarters of the way along the wall on the right.

Through that, veer left by 45 degrees to a squeezer stile after 40 yards and then stay to the right of a wall. A little way beyond another stone barn, a through stile affords access to a walled lane.

Continue forward along this but, by the first bungalow, turn right onto an even broader lane which leads to the main road, the B6270, in the centre of Healaugh, a most attractive hamlet with some pretty stone houses.

Turn left along the road. At the end of the village, and by the end house, turn right into another lane which is signed to Grinton and Reeth. Surprisingly this lane is very short. After a few yards, and through a five-barred gate, it is transformed into an ordinary field path running to the right of a wall.

This leads directly to the banks of the River Swale. There, turn left along the riverside path which continues through a succession of stiles to reach a large suspension bridge spanning the river on the right.

Do not cross the bridge. Instead continue forward through a gate before swinging away from the Swale towards a stile with a five-barred gate alongside.

Beyond this aim leftwards to a small but obvious footbridge. At the far end go left up a walled lane. This climbs gently, swings right through 45 degrees and emerges onto the village green in the centre of Reeth.

3. ARKENGARTHDALE

A low level walk using field and riverside paths to penetrate one of the more remote and quieter valleys of the National Park.

Route:. Reeth – West Rawcroft – Langthwaite – Castle Farm – Reeth.

Distance: 7 miles

Start: The village green, Reeth. Map reference 037993.

Map: Ordnance Survey Outdoor Leisure Map number 30, "Yorkshire Dales, Northern and Central Areas".

Public transport: Bus service number 30 Richmond-Gunnerside-Keld. Daily except Sundays. United Bus Company.

Dalesbus service number 803, Leeds – Harrogate – Reeth – Hawes. Summer Sundays and Bank holidays only. Harrogate and District Bus Company.

Car: Reeth is on the B6270 Richmond – Keld road through Swaledale. There is parking around the village green in Reeth (honesty box).

THE RED LION, LANGTHWAITE

This small but charming country pub is at the half-way point in the walk so providing an ideal stopping place for a drink, a bar meal or both. From it paths radiate in all directions, either along the course of the Arkle Beck or up onto the higher moors which cradle the valley.

It is both unpretentious and homely with cushioned wall seats and flowery curtains. In the bar the beam-and-plank ceiling is very low but even lower in the minute side-snug. Amongst other attractions some pieces of Delft, carved horn beakers and a fox mask reflect the taste of licensee Mrs. Rowena Hutchinson. It has been used for the filming of episodes of the television series, "All Creatures Great and Small".

Walkers are made more than welcome. To cater for their needs Ordnance Survey maps and walking guides are on sale, along with signed copies of books by Wainwright and James Herriot.

Dating from 1600 it has been an inn ever since, so making it one of the oldest pubs in the Yorkshire Dales. Its wide range of bitters includes McEwan's, Younger's Scotch, Theakston's, Webster's Yorkshire and John Smith's Magnet.

Opening Times: Monday to Saturday, 10.30 to 15.00 and 18.30 to 23.00; Sundays: 10.30 to 12.00 for coffee, 12.00 to 15.00 and 19.00 to 22.30. It is closed on Christmas Day.

The Red Lion, Langthwaite

ARKLE BECK

Arkengarthdale has the distinction of being the most northerly of all the Yorkshire Dales. The beck, known as Arkle, travels but a short distance before joining the Swale near Grinton. It rises on the lonely moors leading up to Tan Hill, England's highest pub.

NORSE NAMES

The villages are strung out at intervals up the valley. Their names – Langthwaite, Arkle Town and Whaw – all bear witness to early Norse settlement with little outside influence over subsequent centuries.

LANGTHWAITE

With its tiny cluster of stone houses, a single shop and the Red Lion, Langthwaite is the hub of the valley. Its main distinction is the "Waterloo" church built in 1817 with government money to combat the radical ideas and atheism generated by the French Revolution. Anywhere less radical than Langthwaite is impossible to imagine.

TURNPIKE

The narrow road from Reeth through Arkengarthdale was one of the first to be turnpiked in Yorkshire. This was done mainly to facilitate the transport of coal from several small collieries on the moors around Tan Hill.

THE WALK

Leave the Swaledale village of Reeth by the minor road signed to Arkengarthdale which runs to the right of the Buck Hotel. Stay with it for a little over half a mile. Just beyond a cattle grid and a bend to the left, turn right through a gated stile a few yards to the left of a white gate.

Follow the distinct path as it heads towards a stile on the left and then maintain direction to pass a stone field barn with a red-brick extension.

Continue along the same line over a succession of fields until gaining a through stile with a junction of power lines directly overhead. Keep forward still with one set of wires. Fremington Edge is to the right, Calver Hill to the left.

After going through the next stile, contour across a sloping field to a small gate and cross the bed of a small stream to a footpath sign.

From there, walk in the direction of Langthwaite, soon joining a broad grass track. This narrows as it climbs slightly to a small gate. Beyond

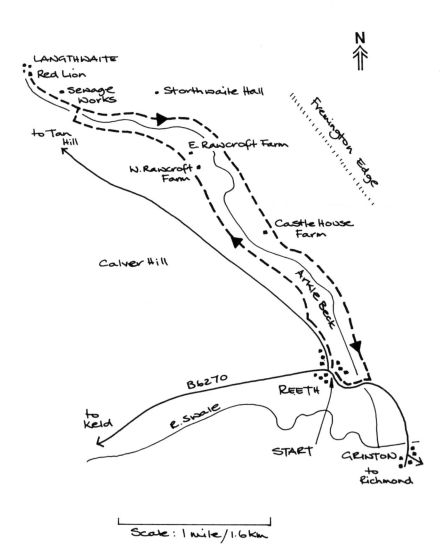

the next two fields join another wide track by a five-barred gate and follow it downhill to the right for a distance of one hundred yards.

By a telegraph pole leave the track to head for a waymarked through stile on the left. Stay with the clear, waymarked path through a succession of fields and meadows dotted with the stone field barns so typical of the Dales and of Swaledale in particular. These, as much as the village names, are proof of the Norse influences in the area because they are a direct historical continuation of the "seter" or mountain pasture tradition still practised by farmers in parts of Norway.

Arkle Beck is a short distance away to the right while beyond it, the slopes of Fremington Edge are littered with the remains of abandoned quarries and lead mine workings.

Eventually the path widens again into a broad, green swathe running a short distance to the left of a wall as it passes above East Rawcroft Farm to another waymarked stile.

From there head for West Rawcroft Farm with its pretty, flower filled garden, unusual for a working farm, and red painted doors. Ignoring waymarks leading off to the right, maintain the line of direction to a broad track before forking right to a waymarked gate.

After this the path initially has a wall to the right as it passes through two gateways before reaching a wood. Skirt to the left of this, negotiating a somewhat muddy section before climbing slightly with an old wire fence to a footpath finger post near a red five-barred gate which carries a "NO ACCESS" notice.

Pass through the wall gap ten yards to the left to follow the waymarked path across a succession of four fields to a gate in the wall on the right. Pass through this and turn left along the bank of Arkle Beck.

Turn right over the first footbridge and then left along a walled lane which passes the sewage disposal plant on its way to the Red Lion in the heart of Langthwaite village.

Suitably refreshed in the Red Lion, retrace your steps as far as the footbridge over Arkle Beck. This time do not cross. Instead keep along the walled lane as it swings away from the beck to run just inside the boundary of a magnificent beech woodland which covers the slope to the left.

While still inside the woods fork right at a Y-junction before dropping to a short tunnel with a stile at the far end. From there enter a shallow valley, pass through a gated stile and reach a footbridge.

The valley of Slei Gill stretching away to the left bears more scars of bygone mining operations with Storthwaite Hall clearly visible.

Continue ahead through a small gate to walk with a wall on the left and Arkle Beck on the right. Beyond the next stile still keep forward to a five-barred gate, resisting any temptation to recross Arkle Beck by another footbridge.

Ten yards beyond that gate veer right, as directed by a footpath sign pointing in the direction of Reeth. Instead of staying with the beck as it goes through a large bend the path, clearly waymarked, veers left over open ground to a stile constructed between two coniferous trees.

From there it crosses more pastureland before gradually climbing away from the beck as it traverses Thorn Dale to arrive at a small gate affording access to a broad track. Cross directly, keeping forward to the left of Castle House Farm before going round by the field edge as directed by a series of yellow arrows.

By the corner of the farmhouse turn left to a waymarked gap and stay forward to a gated stile. Through that drop slightly with a wall on the left before passing to the right of a derelict farm to reach a footpath sign. Beyond this, remain to the left of Arkle Beck, walking along a rocky, winding path which passes through a wall gap before turning right, and then left, almost at once.

Beyond a clump of trees it enters a field. Cross this to another junction. Fork left up a broad track to a five-barred gate. In the next field aim for the gateway with a field barn close by. From there follow a series of white arrows through a succession of stiles to the main road, the B6270.

Turn right along this but exercise extreme caution when crossing Reeth Bridge which is narrow and set at an awkward angle for the traffic. Stay with the road for about a quarter of a mile to regain Reeth village green.

4. GUNNERSIDE GILL

A moderate route which rewards the walker with ever-changing vistas over a never-ending panorama of heather-covered moors. There is also a rich historical interest amongst the ruins of former lead smelting mills.

Route: Gunnerside – Botcher Gill Gate – Gill Head – Birbeck Wood – Gunnerside.

Distance: 7 miles

Start: The King's Head, Gunnerside, Swaledale. Map reference 943982.

Map: Ordnance Survey Outdoor Leisure Map number 30, "Yorkshire Dales, Northern and Central Areas".

Public transport: Bus service number 30, Richmond – Reeth – Gunnerside-Keld. Daily except Sundays. United Bus Company.

Dalesbus service number 803, Leeds – Harrogate – Ripon – Hawes. Summer Sundays and Bank Holidays only. Harrogate and District Bus Company.

Car: Gunnerside is located on the B6270 Richmond to Keld road through Swaledale. Limited parking alongside Gunnerside Beck in the centre of the village.

THE KING'S HEAD, GUNNERSIDE

The King's head is a classic small Dales pub situated in the very heart of this attractive village. The bar is open-plan, subdivided by an arch. The settle seats inside are complemented in good weather by tables and seats outside. William and Elsie Whitehead reserve a special welcome for walkers and maintain a well-stocked bar which includes Theakston's Bitter, XB, Old Peculier and John Smith's Magnet Bitter. The home-cooked food is excellent.

Opening times: Mondays to Friday, 12.00 to 14.00 and 19.00 to 23.00;Saturdays, 11.00 to 15.00 and 19.00 to 23.00; Sunday, 12.00 to 15.00 and 19.00 to 22.30. In summer the hours are flexible and there may be all-day opening.

GUNNERSIDE

The village, built of stone from the surrounding fells, is of Norse origin but reached its peak with the rise of lead mining in the eighteenth and nineteenth centuries. In more recent years it has enjoyed a revival of fortune through the development of tourism.

GUNNERSIDE GILL

Today the gill has a quality of remoteness but there is still sufficient evidence to prove that the valley, flanked by high moorlands, was an important centre of the lead mining industry. In the lonely setting at the head of the gill, the walker will find the remains of smelt mills, spoil heaps and hushes.

For the nature lover there is the constant call of the grouse, curlew and lapwing, all complemented by sightings of the dipper, that chocolate brown bird with the Persil-like chest which loves to perch and bounce on rocks midstream. It is often accompanied by the grey wagtail.

Gunnerside Gill, Gunnerside village

THE WALK

From the King's Head in the centre of Gunnerside head along the B6270 in the direction of Muker. However, almost immediately cross the stone bridge over Gunnerside Beck.

Within a few yards, where the road turns sharply to the left through 90 degrees, stay forward along the minor road which leads to Shoregill Head and Gunnerside Lodge. This probably follows the line of the old Corpse Road (See walk on Fremington Edge).

Beyond the last house, and over the first cattle grid, turn right onto a narrow path which climbs diagonally leftwards up the steep pasture to reach a Y-junction after 80 yards. Fork left to pass between some hawthorn trees.

By this stage the path has become rather indistinct so aim a little to the right of a small stone structure marked on the map as a reservoir.

A short distance higher up than this, and having passed through a small area of shake holes, turn right along a bridleway. This climbs gradually for some distance before levelling out to contour through Gunnerside Pastures below jingle Pot Edge.

This is a former lead miners' track leading to the remains of the old workings which still scar this area of Swaledale. The level walking makes it possible to appreciate the magnificent panorama of moorlands cradling the entire length of Gunnerside Gill with Whin Hall and High Scar prominent across the valley.

The track provides excellent walking for well over a mile before swinging left into Botcher Gill where it reaches a wooden gate before making a U-turn.Within a few yards there is a junction. Fork right onto another wide track.

This runs by Dolly Dead Level before meandering its way through the old spoil heaps of North Hush to begin its final descent into the head of Gunnerside Gill. This section of the route provides a bird's eye perspective of the abandoned workings and their associated buildings nestling by the beckside.

For anyone with time to spare, and an interest in industrial archaeology, it is possible to walk further upstream on good paths to explore more thoroughly this extensive industrial complex from the

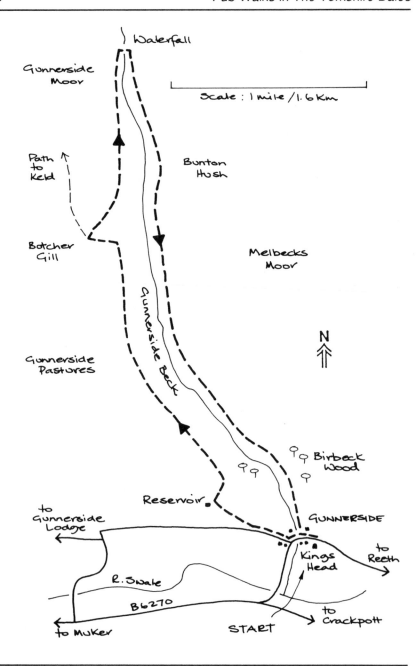

eighteenth and nineteenth centuries. However, our route continues by using the stepping stones to cross the stream issuing from Blakethwaite Gill and then climbing a short flight of stone steps leading to the narrow footbridge over Gunnerside Gill.

From the far end keep just to the left of the ruined building to take the narrow path heading down the valley. After several hundred yards this climbs one hundred feet above the stream and then levels out as it skirts around another ruined building at Bunton Hush.

Continue downstream beneath Swinbank Scar and Melbecks Moor. By a cairn fork right and lose height gradually, soon acquiring a wall on the right. Beyond two stiles the path leads to some attractive riverside pastures which are little more than a rabbit warren of metropolitan proportions.

After a narrow gate, followed by a stile, keep to the left of a wall but, just in front of some trees, turn right through another stile and then immediately left. Within ten yards turn left through another stile which is waymarked.

Continue forward for a short distance but, after crossing a side stream, turn right to climb through a wood to another stile accompanied by a sign which reads, "Footpath. Gunnerside Gill, Woodland Path".

Proceed through Birbeck Wood until the path finally emerges into the open where the beckside banks have been strengthened to prevent flooding, a reminder that these moorland streams are not always gentle.

On reaching the first house on the outskirts of Gunnerside village go round it to the right to reach a small gate. Beyond this there are walls on either side for a distance of 40 yards. Descend a small flight of steps and at the bottom turn left to reach the road directly opposite to the King's Head.

5. KELD

One of the finest walks in Upper Swaledale offering majestic views of the higher valley where the river forms a gigantic bend.

Route: Keld – Kisdon Hill – Muker – Swinner Gill – Keld.

Distance: $5^1/_2$ miles.

Start: Village car park, Keld, Swaledale. Map reference 893012.

Map: Ordnance Survey Outdoor Leisure Map number 30, "Yorkshire Dales, Northern and Central Areas".

Public transport: Bus service number 30, Richmond – Gunnerside – Keld. Tuesdays and Saturdays only. United Bus Company.

Dalesbus service number 803, Leeds-Harrogate-Ripon-Hawes-Keld. Summer Sundays and Bank Holidays only. Harrogate and District Bus Company.

Car: Keld is signed from the B6270 road from Richmond to Tan Hill. There is a small car park in the village (Honesty Box).

THE FARMERS' ARMS

This small, unpretentious pub in the outstandingly attractive village of Muker provides a welcome resting point at the half way stage of this walk, although in summer it may look overcrowded. Despite this the service provided by the joint landlords, G.J. Bridel and J.N. Fawcett, is both speedy and efficient, and also very friendly.

At lunch-time and again in the evenings, excellent if simple fare may be washed down with a choice from Theakston's Bitter, XB or Old Peculier. In addition there is John Smith's Magnet. A recent and very popular addition is Conciliation Ale which is brewed at the new Butterknowle Brewery in Teesdale. The small, cosy square bar is complemented by tables set on the outside verandah.

Opening times:

Summer: Monday, Closed lunch-time, 18.00 to 23.00; Tuesday to Friday, 12.00 to 14.00 and 18.00 to 23.00; Saturday, 12.00 to 23.00; Sunday, 12.00 to 14.00 and 18.00 to 22.30.

Winter: Monday to Thursday, closed lunch time, open 18.00 to 23.00; Friday, 12.00 to 14.00 and 18.00 to 23.00; Saturday, 12.00 to 23.00; Sunday, 12.00 to 14.00 and 18.00 to 22.30.

KELD

Keld is the highest village in Swaledale. Beyond are the high moors leading towards Tan Hill and Mallerstang Edge from which several small streams flow before coming together to form the Swale.

From Keld the scenery changes. The basic limestone gives the valley a gentler image with numerous farms dotting the lower slopes.

Keld, from the Norse name for "village by the river", is little more than a cluster of grey stone houses around a minute square with a couple of chapels and a school.

It flourished in parallel with the lead mining industry but today is a quiet place perhaps best known as a stopping place on the Pennine Way.

KISDON FORCE

Its main tourist attraction is Kisdon Force, a waterfall set in a well-wooded gorge below Kisdon Hill. The best view is to be obtained from the last footbridge over the Swale which is mentioned in the route description.

MUKER

Muker, another Norse name which translates as "cultivated village", is one of the most pretty places in Swaledale. As with so many others its history is tied-up with that of lead mining.

THE WALK

This moderate walk must surely he one of the most satisfying in the whole of England. From the slopes of Kisdon Hill it offers superlative views down Upper Swaledale before the river makes its major turn eastwards near the village of Muker.

From the car park exit in Keld proceed along the lane directly opposite which is signed to Muker. After several hundred yards a Y-junction is

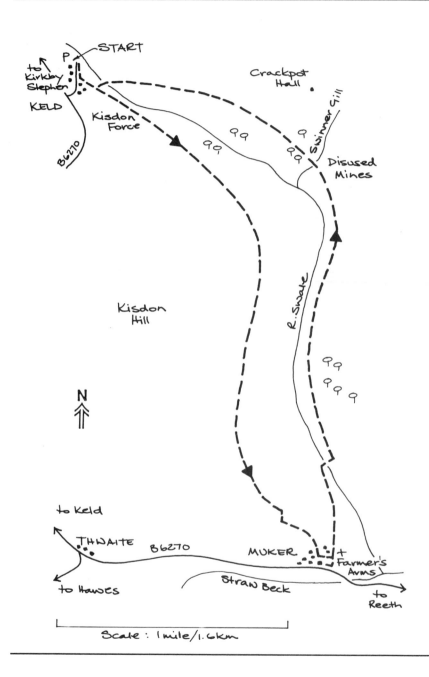

reached with Pennine Way finger posts pointing in both directions: one to the right and one to the left. Fork right.

Soon, through the trees on the left, there is a fleeting glimpse of a local beauty spot, Kisdon Force. The lane develops into a well-trodden path above the Swale as it passes through a five-barred gate to climb by some limestone crags.

On reaching a small cairn, with a Pennine Way sign adjacent, fork right again to continue the climb up the slopes of Kisdon Hill towards another stile which also has a Pennine Way sign alongside.

Turn left on to the path staying close to the right of a wall with the bracken-covered slopes all around. The path is rough and stoney in sections but the reward is a dramatic view across the valley into Swinner Gill with the ruins of Crackpot Hall easy to pinpoint. Ivelet Moor, Black Moor and Hall Moor all add to the grandeur of the scenery.

After a ladder stile, followed by a cairn, the path develops into a wide grass track, the soft, springy turf making for delightful upland walking. Progress is slowed only by two further stiles separated by a five-barred gate.

Sadly, the route soon begins to lose height as it makes towards a further ladder stile. Over this swing left but remain to the right of a wall to a stile. From there the path traverses a meadow to a T-junction by a barn.

A finger post shows the Pennine Way heading off towards the right. Ignore it for this is the parting of the ways. We turn left into a walled lane which is a section of the ancient corpse road from Keld to Grinton (see Gunnerside Gill walk).

Through the next five-barred gate join a bridleway signed to Muker, continuing forward yet again when another bridleway joins ours from the right. After this the track acquires a surface as it descends rapidly into Muker.

On reaching the first house turn right to pass the minuscule Literary Institute, surely the smallest in the country, and then right again along the B6270 to the Farmers' Arms which is set back a little from the road.

Begin the return leg by retracing your steps to pass the Village Stores and swinging left to climb by the Literary Institute and the slightly larger Public Hall.

Literary Institute, Muker

It is worth visiting the small stone church of St. Mary with its simple nave, wooden beam roof and sundial over the west door. Built during the reign of Elizabeth I to serve the upper reaches of Swaledale, it was only the second church in the valley.

By the Post Office turn right and, almost immediately, left to a couple of footpath signs indicating routes to Gunnerside and Keld. Continue between a group of buildings to a through stile by a gate and then follow the well-defined path as it crosses the first field to another stile alongside a gate.

Beyond, go round the corner of a field barn to a through stile and stay with the path as it crosses a series of riverside meadows to emerge onto the bank of the Swale.

Turn right for a few yards and then left over Rampsholme Bridge. At the far end climb a flight of six steps to a T-junction. Turn left along the path signed to Keld.

After a very short climb turn left onto a wider path and, within a further one hundred yards, go left onto a broad track which comes in from the right.

It is now possible to trace the outward route high on the flank of Kisdon Hill by looking across the river to the left.

Continue along the very broad track, yet another created to serve the lead mines. After about a mile it turns right into the mouth of Swinner Gill where it crosses a wooden footbridge. Continue forward through a five-barred gate, climbing a short distance through more lead mining relics, to a junction.

Do not go left. This track is barred by a locked gate and the "NO ACCESS" sign is clearly displayed. Instead, fork right along the rocky track which climbs for more than half a mile to open-up to some exhilarating views of the moorlands surrounding Upper Swaledale.

As the track nears the summit of Stoney Hill another path, coming from Crackpot Hall, forms a junction by coming in from the right. Stay forward and, after a further 20 yards, ignore another green track which forks off to the right.

Follow the main track as it swings through a sharp bend by a barn. At this point there are more spoil heaps , souvenirs of the now defunct lead mining industry. From here, the going levels out but, through the next five-barred gate, the descent commences towards a bridge which is followed within ten yards by a junction.

The footpath signs show both the Pennine Way and the Coast-to-Coast routes. Fork left onto the narrower path which soon leads to a footbridge over the infant Swale.

At the far end turn right to a gate and continue climbing a short distance to a T-junction with more Pennine Way signs pointing in different directions.

Turn right along the lane which leads back to the car park in Keld and formed part of the outward route.

6. SEDBERGH

An easy route, ideal for an afternoon stroll, along the foot of Winder and round the outskirts of the town This allows ample time to explore Sedbergh itself.

Route: Bull Hotel – Settlebeck Gill – Lockbank – – Brimshaw-Rawthey Way – Bull Hotel.

Distance: $4^1/_2$ miles.

Start: Bull Hotel, Sedbergh.Map reference, 659921.

Maps: 1. Ordnance Survey Outdoor Leisure Map number 2, "Yorkshire Dales, Western Area"; 2. Ordnance Survey Landranger Map number 97, "Kendal to Morecambe.

Public transport: Sedbergh is connected with Garsdale station on the Settle to Carlisle line by a daily bus service during August. Cumberland Bus Company and J.Woof.

There is also a bus service linking Sedbergh with Dent and Garsdale stations on summer Sundays. Bus service number 566, Sedbergh-Kirkby Lonsdale. Schooldays only. Cumberland Motor Services Ltd.

A bus service from Bowness to Barnard Castle stops in Sedbergh. Operated Monday to Saturday in August by Cumberland Motors Services Ltd. and J. Woof.

Bus service 564, Sedbergh to Kendal. Daily except Sundays. Operated jointly by Cumberland Motor Services Ltd. and J. Woof.

Car: Sedbergh is on the A684 road from Northallerton to Kendal, five miles east of the M6 motorway.There are two large car parks in or near the town centre.

THE BULL HOTEL

Standing on Main Street in the centre of Sedbergh, the Bull is a former coaching inn that has been modernised. It has two separate bars, the Winder and the Langdale. Both are large and comfortable. Landlord Harry Wilkinson carries a wide range of ales, all on handpump, including Boddington's Bitter, Castle Eden Bitter, Whitbread's Trophy and Chester's Mild. Bar meals are available, there is a separate restaurant and en-suite accommodation is available.

Opening times: Monday to Wednesday, 12.00 to 15.00 and 18.30 to 23.00; Thursday to Friday, 11.30 to 15.00 and 16.30 to 23.00; Saturday, 11.00 to 15.00 and 18.30 to 23.00; Sunday, 12.00 to 15.00 and 19.00 to 22.30.

The Bull Hotel

SEDBERGH

Sedbergh, with a population of 2,500, is the largest town within the Yorkshire Dales National Park although, since local government reorganisation in 1974, it has been incorporated in the county of Cumbria.

The name is derived from the Norse, "Setberg", translated as "Flat Topped Hill", an obvious reference to the rounded fells of the Howgills which shield the town on its northern side.

The Normans built a motte and bailey castle on Castleshaw in the north-eastern corner of the town but little now remains except grassy mounds. The Parish church is also Norman while the market, still held every Wednesday on Joss Lane car park, has been functioning since the grant of a charter in 1251.

Apart from livestock, the town's wealth was based on the textile industry, especially hand knitting. The narrow alleys crammed between Main Street and Back Street, once boasted wooden galleries on their first stories where, as in nearby Dent, the knitters sat while working.

In the eighteenth century cotton mills were built at Birks, Millthrop and Howgill and a woollen mill at Hebblethwaite.

Above all, however, Sedbergh is famous for its school whose playing fields cover large areas on the southern side of the town. It was established in 1525 by Roger Lupton, a native of the area and Provost of Eton. It was rebuilt in 1716 (the old building is used a library and museum) and became a Public School in 1874.

THE WALK

From the Bull Hotel follow the one-way traffic system along Main Street for a little over 100 yards. Immediately before the car park make a left turn into Joss Lane, climbing moderately while following frequent signs "To The Fell".

Beyond the last houses pass through a five-barred gate. At a Y-junction ten yards further on go left along the broad track as it passes well to the left of a farm house to a gated stile accompanied by a yellow waymark.

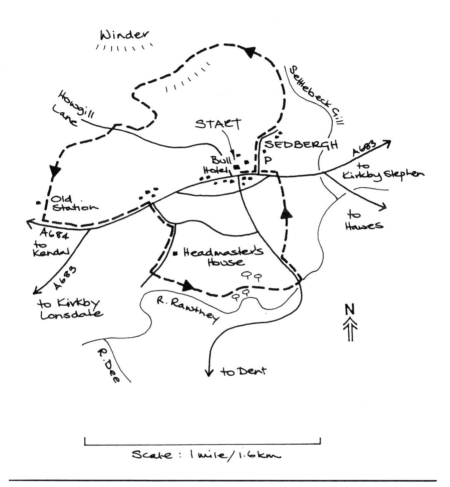

Scale : 1 mile / 1.6 km

Over this the track narrows into a path enclosed initially between a hedgerow and a wall. Beyond a second stile it begins a steeper ascent with Settlebeck Gill on the immediate right. Go through an old-fashioned metal kissing gate, turn through 45 degrees to the left and pass behind a bench onto a broad, green track climbing through a spread of bracken and gorse up the southern flank of Winder, one of the Howgill fells. Do not take the path just to the right of the wall. The summit is not the objective. After 100 yards turn left with the path as it narrows to run along the 260 metre contour. There is a T.V. mast and tiny reservoir down below on the left. The town of Sedbergh is also spread out below and there are more distant views of Middleton Fell and up the length of Barbondale.

At the next Y-junction fork left, gradually losing height until joining another path along the wall of Lockbank Farm.

Turn left through the first five-barred gate, continue forward through a second after ten yards and swing right between the farm buildings to a third.

From there follow the driveway to gain Howgill Lane by an acute bend. Turn right onto this, heading away from Sedbergh. Pass two stone houses almost at once, "The Mount" on the right and "Highlands" on the left. 100 yards after joining the lane turn through the first five-barred gate on the left and advance on the left-hand side of a wall, followed by a fence.

Initially a sea of well pounded mud obscures the path but soon there is a broad green rutted track to follow. Stay along this until reaching a corner on the right where the fence becomes a wall. Turn sharp right, alongside the wall, pass a yellow waymark on a tree and cross a stream to a five-barred gate. Through this turn left, walking to the right of the stream and another fence.

Negotiate two stiles within 12 yards of each other but, where fence and stream go to the left, maintain general line of direction across open pasture to a walled bank surmounted by a hedgerow.

Turn left onto a path running along the base of this embankment. Beyond two five-barred gates the path widens into a track at the site of a former station on the disused railway from Kirkby Lonsdale to Penrith.

Stay along the track until the main A684 road between Sedbergh and Kendal. Turn left along this for half a mile, passing the junction with the Kirkby Lonsdale road. By the cemetery turn right into Busk Lane which is signed to Dent. Take the first road on the right, soon passing "Berksholme", the home of the Headmaster of Sedbergh School as the road heads for the hamlet of Birks.

By the gateway of the first house on the outskirts of the hamlet make a left turn through a kissing gate onto a path signed as part of the

Rawthey Way. At first it runs to the right of a hedge, quickly coming to a Y-junction. Fork right down the slope towards the River Rawthey and a stile. Over this stay forward along the perimeter of a rugby pitch, with the river on the right. ⋅

Over another stile veer left away from the river, climbing through a wall gap and staying a little to the left of an octagonal tower before going leftwards to a seat.

Continue outside the wood for 100 yards before turning right through a gate. Walk diagonally leftwards, following a vague path through the trees to another gate. Stay close to the left-hand boundary of the next field on a well used path to meet the Sedbergh-Dent road at Millthrop Mill bridge.

Turn left along the road but, by the 30 mph signs, turn right through a gate onto another field path signed to Back Lane and Settlebeck. This crosses a large field to a gated stile and a Y-junction just beyond.

Fork left to a through stile after five yards. Then stay to the left of the boundary wall of a large house to a kissing gate. Cross the driveway to a second kissing gate and stay forward to a third by the entrance to "The Old Vicarage".

Stay forward along a wider track to reach the junction of Back Lane and Main Street. Turn left along Main Street for the Bull Hotel.

7. DENTDALE

Based on one of the most picturesque villages in the Dales, this walk encompasses both high moorland and riverside paths. There is one long steep climb.

Route: Dent – Flinter Gill – Green Lane – Nun House – Mill Bridge – Dent.

Distance: 5 miles

Start: Sun Inn, Dent. Map reference 705871

Map: Ordnance Survey Outdoor Leisure Map number 2, "Yorkshire Dales, Western Area".

Public transport: Dent station is on the Settle-Carlisle line but is about five miles from the village. There is a connecting bus service on summer Sundays. For current time-table see "Dales Connections".

Bus service number 565, Sedbergh-Dent-Lea Yeat. Schooldays only. Cumberland Motor Services.

Car: Dent is reached by a minor road signed from Sedbergh. Other, unclassified roads, provide links with Ingleton, Hawes and Kirkby Lonsdale.

There is a large Yorkshire Dales National Park car park on the edge of the village.

THE SUN INN, DENT

The attractive white-fronted Sun Inn has stood in the centre of the tiny village of Dent since the 1630's but it has not always been a pub.. In the words of landlord Martin Stafford, "It has had a chequered history".

Not surprising, then, that it has some splendid and ancient oak beams and timbers, some studded with coins.The walls are liberally decorated with photographs of the Yorkshire Dales. Seating is on dark brown arm chairs and brown leatherette wall benches. In winter there is always a welcoming open log fire while in summer rustic benches and tables are placed outside.

The Sun is closely associated with the new Dent Brewery, established in a converted barn some three miles higher up Dentdale, which now brews in the order of a thousand gallons a week.

The Sun offers Dent Bitter and Ram's Bottom Strong Ale, a drink to be enjoyed *after* the walk. In addition it serves Theakston's XB.

There is a wide range of bar meals and overnight accommodation.

Opening times: Monday to Thursday, 11.00 to 14.30 and 19.00 to 23.00; Friday and Saturday, 11.00 to 14.30.and 18.15 to 23.00; Sunday, 12.00 to 15.00 and 19.00 to 22.30.

DENT

Time is required to explore what is probably the most interesting and attractive of all the villages within the Yorkshire Dales National Park.

For one of those unfathomable bureaucratic reasons, Dent was transferred from the West Riding of Yorkshire to Cumbria as a result of the local government reorganisation of 1974. Perhaps suspecting that this will prove nothing more than a temporary arrangement, the new County Council has so far failed to remove several roadside boundary stones carrying the legend "WR" or "West Riding".

Despite this momentous change, however, Dent village remains within the Yorkshire Dales National Park.

It is the only significant settlement within the Dee valley, testimony to its Norse origins because the Vikings preferred to live in scattered farmsteads.

The village is a cluster of colour-washed stone cottages flanking narrow cobbled streets. It has two pubs and several cafes. In recent years it has developed into a tourist honeypot but, out of season it is a quiet place with fewer than 600 inhabitants. This has not always been the case. In 1801 it boasted 1,773. Then it was a place of some significance noted chiefly as a centre of the textile industry.

Its chief products were gloves and stockings made by the "Terrible Knitters of Dent". This title was accorded to the women, not because of their tempers or other failings, but because of the speed with which they plied their needles. They were allegedly so fast that sparks flew.

Dent village

This industry peaked during the seventeenth, eighteenth and nineteenth centuries when wooden galleries were attached to houses at first floor level. Within these the knitters sat carrying on their trade until the coming of machinery rendered them redundant.

ADAM SEDGEWICK

Dent is also famous as the birthplace of Adam Sedgewick. His father was rector there and also master of the tiny grammar school which still stands in the churchyard.

Adam progressed through nearby Sedbergh School before going on to Cambridge where he eventually became a professor. Today he is recognised as the father of modern geology, much of his field work being carried out in the dales.

A fountain, set in Shap granite, stands in the centre of Dent as a memorial to the village's most famous son.

DENT STATION

Dent's other claim to fame is its railway station on the Settle to Carlisle railway. Standing some 1, 150 feet above sea level it is the highest main line station in England.

DENT MARBLE

This is a grey fossiliferous limestone which, when polished, becomes very attractive. In Victorian times it was in great demand for use as fireplace surrounds, table-tops and ornaments. It has long been out of fashion.

A fine example may be seen in the parish church of St. Andrew where the floor between the choir stalls and sanctuary is paved with this local product.

THE WALK

Turn left out of the Sun Inn walking along the cobbled village street to the Yorkshire Dales National Park car park. There turn left again into the narrow street opposite recognised by the arrow signing "The Shop on the Green".

Pass the rear of the Sun Inn and stay to the right of the village green before maintaining direction to enter another narrow road signed to Flintergill Outrake. Beyond Ghyl Head House this becomes a rough bridleway climbing very steeply through woodland with Flintergill Beck rushing down on the left.

Beyond the second five-barred gate there is a stone barn on the right and, shortly afterwards, a waterfall cascading over enormous stone slabs.

On leaving the trees the track develops into a walled lane traversing high ground at an easier gradient. After a mile from Dent it forms a T-junction with Green Lane, another walled track running along the contour. Turn left along this.

Almost at once there is an excellent view of Rise Hill and Aye Gill Pike to the north of Dentdale while, in the distance ahead, Great Knoutberry Hill is prominent.

More immediately to the left is a series of abandoned quarries from which Dent Marble was extracted until the early years of this century.

Continue along Green Lane for more than a mile as it runs below Little Combe Hill to another T-junction. At this point the enormous hulk of Whernside is more or less directly ahead on the far side of Deepdale.

Turn left along the new walled lane which is signed to Nun House and Outrake. Height is lost rapidly. After passing to the left of a small conifer plantation and then to the right of High Nun House, the track

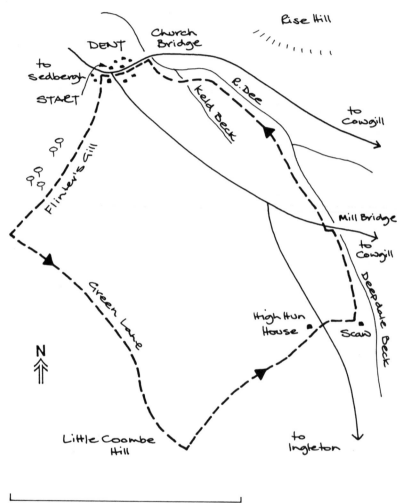

Scale : 1 mile/1.6 km

makes a rendezvous with the minor road through Deepdale which links Dent with Ingleton.

Cross directly onto another broad track signed as a footpath to Mill Bridge. Within 10 yards pass through a gate, cross a farm driveway to a second gate with a footpath sign alongside, and then continue forward to the left of two tall trees. After a further 25 yards proceed through a gateway before going to the left of a wall and hedge to yet another gate. Through this swing sharp left, as signed, to gain a stile by the corner of a cottage at Scow Farm

Over that aim for the waymarked finger post in the centre of the field before heading-off to the far right-hand corner where there is another obvious footpath finger post. Stay forward over the stile, heading for two trees carrying yellow waymarks.

Beyond, keep just to the left of the line of trees to another stile. From this point the path is clear and easy to follow but after 75 yards veer towards the right by a hawthorn tree heading closer to Deepdale Beck.

By a faded unofficial sign saying "footpath", turn right through the trees to gain the beckside and a gated stile by Mill Bridge which carries the minor road from Dent to Cowgill. The mill was one of three which used to operate in the valley.

Do not cross the bridge.Instead turn left along the road for 15 yards and then right on to a path signed to Church Bridge. After 25 yards turn sharp right for four yards and then sharp left, walking between a wire fence on the left and Deepdale Beck on the right.

It is soon obvious that this path through delightful riverside pastures is well used. Notice, too, that for the maim part the field boundaries in Dentdale are hedgerows rather than stone, a certain sign that the climate in the valley is milder than in some other parts of the Dales.Most are still maintained by the traditional method of laying which guarantees that they remain stockproof.

After a ladder stile followed by two gated stiles the path passes the confluence of Deepdale Beck and the River Dee. Soon afterwards the squat, square tower of Dent church comes into view ahead.

A short distance from Dent village the Dee arcs through 90 degrees to the left and, initially, the path accompanies it. However, after the next stile and by a derelict barn, turn to the left to cross a wide concrete footbridge spanning Keld Beck. Immediately turn to the right, walking to the left of the beck to gain another stile after 50 yards.

Maintain direction for a further 40 yards, negotiate two stiles separated by five yards and then pass the confluence of Keld Beck with the River Dee.

Remain alongside the river before climbing the flight of steps by Church Bridge. At the top, turn left along the road for the short distance into the village and the Sun Inn.

Church Bridge, Dent

8. HARDRAW FORCE

An easy route offering outstanding views of Upper Wensleydale and a visit to England's highest waterfall above ground.

Route: Hawes – Sedbusk – Simonstone – Hardraw – Brunt Acres Road – Hawes.

Start: National Park Car Park, Hawes. Map reference 876899.

Distance: 4$^1/_2$ miles.

Map: The Ordnance Survey Outdoor Leisure Map number 30, "Yorkshire Dales, Northern and Central Areas".

Public transport: Bus service number 26, Hawes – Leyburn – Richmond. Daily except Sundays. United Bus Company.

Bus service number 159, Hawes – Leyburn – Ripon. Daily except Sundays. United Bus Company.

Dalesbus service number 800, Harrogate/Leeds – Hawes – Keld. Tuesdays in late July and August and Saturdays late July to the end of September. Keighley and District Bus Company.

Dalesbus service number 809, Keighley – Richmond. Tuesdays only in late July and August. Keighley and District Bus Company. Askrigg – Hawes – Garsdale Station to connect with trains on the Settle-Carlisle railway. Saturdays only from mid-July to the end of September. Central Coaches.

Askrigg – Hawes – Garsdale Station to connect with trains on the Settle to Carlisle line. Sundays from May until late September. J.Woof and Company.

For details of other services linking Hawes with Garsdale Station, telephone Wensleydale (0969) 667450.

Car: Hawes is situated on the A684 Sedbergh to Leyburn road. It may also be reached by the minor road from Swaledale over the Buttertubs pass.

Hawes is connected with the A65 by the B6255 through Ingleton. From Settle it may be approached via the B6479 which joins the B6255 at Ribblehead.

The large National Park car park in the former station yard is signed from all the approaches to Hawes and from the centre.

THE GREEN DRAGON, HARDRAW

The Green Dragon Inn is one of the oldest watering holes in the Dales. There is recorded evidence to prove that it occupied the same location in the early 1500s and there is a probability that there was an inn on the site some 300 years earlier.

It appears to have been initially established as a grange or lodging house for the monks of Fountains Abbey when they visited the area to carry out checks on their flocks of sheep.

The unusual name does not owe its existence to some fierce creature which once lived there but rather to the green dragon to be found on the flag or standard that was raised there as a rallying point for the local men reporting for their 40 days of liege service throughout feudal times.

With all this history is there a ghost? Landlady Renee Shay believes there is definitely a "presence" – that of an elderly lady.

Appropriately for such a remote hamlet the building has thick, unplastered stone walls and the bar must be the only one in the country with a genuine, old-fashioned York range. Not surprisingly, when I called on a bitterly cold December day, it had a roaring log fire. On the other hand it was surprising to find that the flagged floors had been carpeted, especially as the Green Dragon is used extensively by walkers, including thousands of Pennine Wayfarers many of whom take advantage of the overnight accommodation it provides or the bar meals it serves.

The Green Dragon serves Theakston's Bitter, XB and Old Peculier all on handpump.

Opening times: Daily, except Christmas Day and Boxing Day, 12.00 to 23.00. It is open even earlier for people to pass through to visit the Hardraw Force (Charge, currently, of 50 pence).

The Green Dragon, Hardraw

HAWES

Today Hawes is a busy, bustling place, the highest market place in Yorkshire and the natural centre of Upper Wensleydale. Surrounded on three sides by high moorland it is a natural communications centre with roads radiating out to Ingleton and Settle through Widdale, to Sedbergh over Garsdale Head and to Keld and Swaledale via the Buttertubs Pass. Two roads, one north Of the River Ure and one south, link it with Leyburn.

Yet, until as recently as 1699 when it was granted a market charter, it was inferior to Gayle which is thought to occupy the site of a Celtic settlement. The name of Hawes is derived from the Anglo-Saxon "haus", which means a pass through the hills, after the fashion of Honister Hause in Cumbria.

It began to flourish in 1599 when it was granted its first market charter, soon spelling the death knell to the older markets at Askrigg and Carperby lower down the valley. The weekly market continues on

Tuesdays while the annual autumn livestock sales generate sales worth several million pounds.

Hawes' supremacy was further enhanced when the Lancaster to Richmond road was turnpiked in the eighteenth century. This led to the building of several coaching Inns which today serve the walker and the tourist. Hawes is also famous for the creamery which produces Wensleydale cheese, originally manufactured from ewe's milk by the monks of Fountains Abbey and, later, by farmers' wives. Hawes is one of the few places where it is possible to see ropemaking in the traditional manner at the premises of R.Outhwaite by the entrance to the old station car park.

Although now closed, the arrival of the railway in 1878 further emphasised the eminence of Hawes, bringing in the first tourists. The former station has now been developed as the Upper Dales Folk Museum with attractive displays of local life in bygone days.

Cocketts Hotel, in the town centre, was formerly a Quaker rest house and a little to the north of the roundabout is the burial ground which has belonged to the Society of Friends since 1680.

HARDRAW FORCE

Hardraw Force may only be approached through the Green Dragon Inn. Dropping almost 100 feet into the centre of a natural rock amphitheatre, it is the highest waterfall above ground in England. By the approach path there is a circular stone bandstand where the annual Hardraw Brass Band contest is held every September as it has been since 1881.

The renowned French tightrope walker, Blondin, crossed over the fall on a tightrope prior to his more publicised feat of crossing Niagara. The artist Turner painted the falls and another famous visitor was the poet William Wordsworth.

THE WALK

Exit from the National Park car park in the converted station yard, Hawes, by crossing the trackbed of the disused railway and continuing up the platform approach which leads to Brunt Acres Road. Turn right along this.

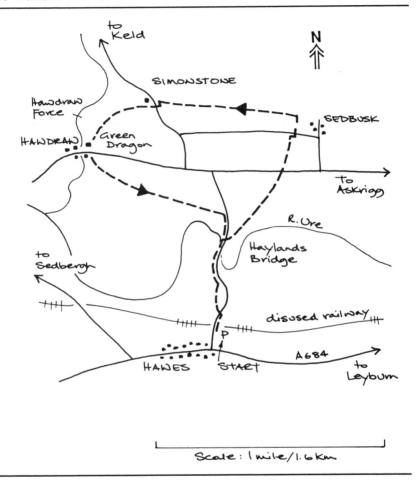

Scale: 1 mile/1.6 km

Within 150 yards, cross the entrance to the new Hawes Rural Workshops complex to negotiate a stile on the left signed "Pennine Way". Follow the flagged path across the large field to a kissing gate which affords a return onto Brunt Acres Road.

Turn left along the road again to cross the impressive Haylands Bridge spanning the River Ure and, about 100 yards beyond take the gated stile on the right.

The path, signed to Sedbusk, veers slightly left to a small footbridge before climbing to another gated stile. Beyond, stay well to the right of a large stone house to arrive at the minor road linking Hawes with Askrigg.

Cross to a gated stile, the path again being signposted to Sedbusk. Climb in a straight line to the crown of the small hill and a gated stile, before descending slightly to a ladder stile and climbing first to the right of a stone barn and then to the left of a wall to gain Sedbusk Lane, almost on the outskirts of Sedbusk hamlet.Turn right along the lane for 10 yards and then left over a stile with a sign to Simonstone adjacent.

Head to a through stile in the left-hand corner of the narrow field which is about 90 yards distant.Turn left through the stile before continuing in a straight line over a number of narrow fields by means of a succession of stiles and gateways. There is also a number of field barns that are so typical of this area of the Yorkshire Dales.

The gentle, easy walking on springy turf allows ample opportunity to enjoy the fine views of Hawes to the left, High Clint limestone scar to the right and of the rising moorlands towards Garsdale Head directly in front.

After two successive ladder stiles, the path develops into a farm driveway which continues, still in a straight line, as far as the minor road at Simonstone opposite Nova Farm.

Turn left for 15 yards and then right into the driveway leading to Simonstone Hall, now a hotel and restaurant serving Theakston's. Opposite the entrance to the hotel go left onto an unsigned but clearly visible path which crosses two fields immediately to the left of a wall. By a stone house swing left, as directed by a sign, dropping down the hill to a stile and the entrance to Hardraw village by the Green Dragon.

Pass through the pub, paying the small admission charge, onto the well-maintained path leading the Hardraw Force. Return by the same route.

From the Green Dragon cross the road onto a farm drive immediately to the right of the Coach House cafe. After 20 yards, and by a wall corner, go left onto a flagged path signed as the Pennine Way to Brunt Acres Road.

Flagged for much of the way, this path traverses a series of meadows with a view of Wether Fell beyond Hawes. On reaching Brunt Acres Road turn right and, having recrossed Haylands Bridge, retrace your steps along the outward route.

Hardraw Force

9. SEMERWATER

This route follows the line of a Roman road onto the high moorlands before descending to one of the only two natural lakes in the Yorkshire Dales.

Route: Bainbridge – Priest Bank – Hawes End – Countersett – Semerwater – Bracken Hill – Bainbridge.

Distance: $5^1/_2$ miles.

Start: Rose and Crown Hotel, Bainbridge, Wensleydale. Map reference 935904

Map: Ordnance Survey Outdoor Leisure Map number 30, "Yorkshire Dales, Northern and Central Areas".

Public transport:

Bus service number 26, Hawes – Leyburn – Richmond. Daily except Sunday. United Bus Company.

Bus service number 159, Hawes – Leyburn – Ripon. Daily except Sundays. United Bus Company.

Dalesbus service number 800, Harrogate/Leeds – Keld. Tuesdays in late July and August and Saturdays and Sundays late July to the end of September. Keighley and District Bus Company.

Dalesbus service number 809, Keighley – Richmond. Tuesdays only in late July and August. Keighley and District Bus Company.

Askrigg – Hawes – Garsdale Station to connect with trains on the Settle – Carlisle line. Summer Sundays only. J. Woof and Company.

Car: Bainbridge is on the A684 Hawes-Leyburn road. There is limited parking by the village green and at the Rose and Crown for patrons only.

THE ROSE AND CROWN, BAINBRIDGE

Situated by the attractive, sloping village green with its stocks, the Rose and Crown, Bainbridge, dates from the fifteenth century. As with so many hostelries in Wensleydale it benefited from the building of the

Lancaster to Richmond turnpike in the eighteenth century when it became a convenient coaching inn. Subsequently it acquired a reputation as "The Pride of Wensleydale".

That distinction is still maintained. There is a small, square cosy lounge bar with ancient wooden beams and panelled walls where, in winter, a crackling open fire blazes merrily in the fireplace with its large stone surround.

Antique cushioned settles line the walls which are decorated with stag heads, copperware, brassware and stuffed fish in glass cases. There is also a tiny snug and a larger public bar which is more sparsely furnished.

The bar menu is not only extensive but enterprising and there is bed and breakfast for anyone wishing to extend their stay.

Beers from the pump include Younger's Scotch Bitter, John Smith's Bitter and John Smith's Magnet.

Opening times: Monday to Friday, 11.30 to 15.00 and 18.30 to 23.00; Saturday, 11.30 to 23.00; Sunday, 12.00 to 15.00 and 19.00 to 22.30

BAINBRIDGE

The Romans arrived in Bainbridge about 80 A.D. and stayed for almost three centuries during which time they constructed a succession of forts on Brough Hill, a grassy mound to the east of the present village and clearly visible from the final section of this walk.

Their forts not only kept the local tribes in order, but helped to protect the Roman investment in the lead mining industry. From Bainbridge a number of Roman roads radiated out principally in the direction of Wharfedale and further west to Ingleton and Lancaster.

Occasionally the custom of horn-blowing at dusk between September 27th and Shrovetide is carried out, a reminder of the period when Bainbridge was part of the Forest of Wensleydale and it was customary to guide hunters down from the fells.

There is no parish church in the village but there is a Friends' Meeting House and a chapel. Today, it houses the northern offices of the Yorkshire Dales National Park.

SEMERWATER

A clay dam, left by a retreating glacier during the ice ages, impounds the water in what is said to be Yorkshire's largest natural lake and one of only two in the Dales, the other being Malham Tarn. In summer it is a mecca for picnickers and is also popular with windsurfers, anglers, canoers and boaters. In winter it is a haven for waterfowl.

Cradled by surrounding moorlands and dominated by the nearby peak of Addleborough at 1,564 feet above sea level, Semerwater is one of the most delectable spots in the Dales. It is drained by the Bain which, at two miles in length, is officially England's shortest river.

Not surprisingly Semerwater's lonely winter setting has spawned a strange legend of a weary traveller arriving in the village asking for food and shelter. He was spurned by all except for one poor shepherd and his wife. As in all good stories of this kind he laid a curse:

"Semerwater rise, Semerwater sink
And swallow all the town
Save yon little house
Where they gave me food and drink"

Semerwater on a brooding late December day

No sooner had the words parted his lips than the heavens opened, an enormous deluge swamping the village and leaving behind the present lake.

Believe the tradition or not, but it is a matter of recorded fact that when the level of the water was deliberately lowered in the 1930s as part of a flood alleviation scheme, a bronze age village was brought to light.

COUNTERSETT

Countersett, the village perched high above Semerwater, is of Norse origin. The second part of its name corresponds with the modern Norwegian word "Seter", which means "upland pasture". As in the Dales, these are still used for summer pasture and usually have wooden barns and huts for the shepherds.

Again, typical of so many other villages in the northern dales, Countersett has a strong Quaker tradition, still retaining its Friends' Meeting House. Some of the other buildings, including the Hall with its mullioned windows and twin-storey porch, date back to the seventeenth century.

THE WALK

From the Rose and Crown and the village green enter the minor road signposted to Countersett, soon passing to the left of the Temperance Hall. The climbing is steep but open country is soon reached with the reward of ever-extending view both up and down the length of Wensleydale.

After half a mile, and where the road bends round to the left, continue forward along an unsigned walled lane with a rough surface. This is Cam High Road, the old Roman road linking the fort at Bainbridge with Ingleton. Continue along this as the climbing eases by Priest Bank to traverse Bainbridge High Pasture for more than a mile.

200 yards before Four Lane Ends, where the Cam High Road intersects the surfaced Hawes to Countersett road, turn left through an inconspicuous gated stile with a weathered waymark alongside.

The path is not easy to trace on the ground so, climb the slope leftwards, aiming for the point where the roadside wall reaches the

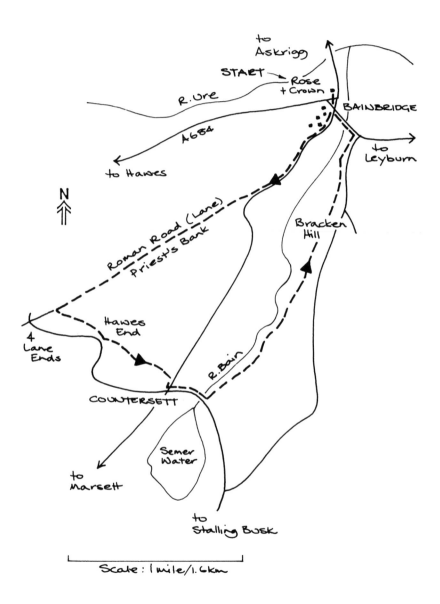

crest of the hill. In bad weather, or for anyone anxious not to make a mistake, it is easier to continue along Cam High Road to Four Lane Ends before making a left turn onto the road in the direction of Countersett.

The path reaches a through stile giving access to the road with a sign to Horton Gill Bridge. Turn left along the road for approximately 150 yards to Hawes End, recognised as the point where the road bends sharply to the right and by a small, abandoned quarry on the left.

At Hawes End turn left through a five-barred gate onto a path signed to Countersett. This clings close to a wall on the right as it drops down the slope and through the reeds to a step stile. Over that continue forward through a very shallow valley for 30 yards before emerging for a first glimpse of Semerwater a long way down below.

20 yards beyond the end of the valley swing diagonally left towards a barn in the adjacent field. Pass a fenced-off spring and cross a stream by a tiny flagged footbridge to a through stile. Turn sharp right and, keeping the barn on the left, descend steeply down the centre of the pasture, aiming some 20 yards to the right of a second barn.

At the bottom cross another stream to a through stile followed, within a yard, by a traditional one. Keep forward over a slight crest before dropping down to a five-barred gate near Countersett Hall. Turn right along a track for 20 yards to reach a road. Turn right along this to meet a junction after a further ten yards. Follow the road round to the left in the direction of Stalling Busk. There is a very steep gradient down to Countersett Bridge which marks the start of the River Bain.

By the far end of the attractive stone bridge make a left turn onto the riverside path. At this point the Bain is calm and tranquil, more reminiscent of a lowland river as it flows through reed-fringed banks in a wide valley. However, as it nears Bainbridge it changes character, developing into a noisy, tumbling affair as it cascades over a series of stone shelves before reaching its confluence with the River Ure.

At the second stile ignore a signposted path to the right, opting instead to remain alongside the river bank which is peppered with mole hills. Along this stretch, too, the keen-eyed observer may spot fox droppings, hovering kestrels, snipe and lapwing, even in winter when the temperatures may be well below zero in the middle of the day.

Where the river sweeps sharply away to the left go over a ladder stile, with a footpath finger post alongside, to climb away from the Bain on a clear, grassy path traversing open meadowland to a through stile.

Maintain direction with a fence on the right to another stile before staying to the left of a barn to a step stile. Advance a further 50 yards, with a wall on the right, to a footpath sign where the wall corners away to the right.

Taking direction from the arm of the sign climb over the crest of Bracken Hill, at a height of 311 metres, before descending to a gate in a wall corner.

Through that the path is again a clear, distinctive green track running through upland pasture. It offers springy turf to make walking a real pleasure and progress rapid. At intervals there are waymarks and always some splendid views.

Shortly after passing to the right of a large walled enclosure with a barn inside the perimeter, veer right downhill to meet a wall flanking Blean Lane, the surfaced road from Bainbridge to Stalling Busk.

At the wall turn left, as signed, to walk just to the left of the road as it drops steeply down to meet the A684 on the outskirts of Bainbridge village. Turn left for the final quarter of a mile to the village green and the Rose and Crown.

10. ASKRIGG

A fortified medieval farmhouse is the focal point of this route which traverses gentle countryside in the heart of Wensleydale.

Route: Askrigg – Nappa Scar – Nappa Hall – Nappa Mill – Worton Bridge – Askrigg.

Distance: 2$^1/_2$ miles

Start: The Kings Arms Hotel, Askrigg, Wensleydale. Map reference 949911.

Map: Ordnance Survey Outdoor Leisure Map number 30, "Yorkshire Dales, Northern and Central Areas".

Public transport:

Bus service number 26, Hawes – Leyburn – Richmond. Daily except Sundays. United Bus Company.

Bus service number 159, Hawes – Leyburn – Ripon. Daily except Sundays. United Bus Company.

Askrigg – Hawes – Garsdale Station to connect with trains on the Settle to Carlisle railway line. Saturdays only from mid-July to the end of September. Central Coaches.

Askrigg – Hawes – Garsdale Station to connect with trains on the Settle to Carlisle railway line. Sundays only from mid-May to the end of September. J.Woof.

Car: Askrigg is located on the unclassified road which runs eastwards from Hawes on the northern side of Wensleydale. It may also be reached from the A684 from Bainbridge from where it is signed. There is limited parking by the church.

THE KING'S ARMS HOTEL

One unique feature of the Kings' Arms Hotel in Askrigg is the glass-fronted gallery looking down into the main bar. Another is the large wooden panel onto which is painted a copy of the poem, "August Dales" by Glynne Hughes.

The fire, which always blazes away on cold winter days, is laid on a griddle which is set in the centre of the enormous fireplace with its stone surround. Behind the flames is a cast iron plate bearing the royal coat of arms.

The pub, which stands in Askrigg's ancient market square, was built in 1760 by John Pratt, a highly successful racehorse owner and trainer, as a manor house with a complex of stables.In 1810 the stables were converted into a coaching inn on the Richmond to Lancaster turnpike.

One of its most illustrious guests was the artist, Turner, who lodged there during a painting tour of the Dales. In more recent times it has been featured in the television series, "All Creatures Great and Small".

The King's Arms

The main bar has a flagged, partially carpeted floor. The beamed ceiling is festooned with various items of equine equipment and a collection of animal traps. The padded wall benches are subdivided into compartments while the walls are decorated with stags' heads, hunting prints and other local pictures.

In addition to serving a wide selection of bar meals, the King's Arms also has a very fine restaurant and provides en-suite accommodation.

There is also a small, low-beamed and oak-panelled front bar with some side snugs and a green marble fireplace. The third bar, at the rear, is flagstoned and more simply furnished. It has a fruit machine and is used for darts, shove-ha'penny, cribbage and dominoes. In summer there are chairs and tables on the two-tiered court yard.

Beers: Newcastle Exhibition, McEwan's 80 Shilling, Younger's Number 3, Tetley's Bitter and Ind Coope Burton.

Opening times: Monday to Friday, 11.00 to 16.00 and 18.30 to 23.00; Saturday, 11.00 to 23.00; Sunday, 12.00 to 16.00 and 18.30 to 22.30

ASKRIGG

With Ellerkin Scar and Askrigq Common as a backdrop, the village of Askrigg sits astride the minor road which links Hawes and Leyburn on the northern side of Wensleydale. This widens by the fifteenth century church to form the cobbled market place complete with stone cross and iron bull-ring set into the cobbles. Askrigg's prosperity was originally based on its market but when this declined with the development of Hawes the village flourished as a centre of clock making and textiles, principally hosiery.It also became an important staging-post on the Richmond to Lancaster Turnpike.

Its former wealth is reflected in the rows of stone-built, three storey houses which flank its streets. Cringley House by the market square was used as Skeldale House for the television series, "All Creatures Great and Small".

THE WALK

From the Kings Arms walk up the main street of Askrigg and, at the junction, follow it round towards the right in the direction of Carperby and Leyburn.

A few yards beyond the entrance to Low Gate, the narrow side road signed to Worton, pass through a stile on the right. Cross the first field by keeping to the left of a stone barn and, subsequently, of a wall to reach a stile. The second field is long and narrow. Remain to the left of a wall and of a second barn to yet another stile set some ten yards to the left of a third barn.

In the third field continue to a waymarked gated stile before advancing, still to the left of a wall but to the right of another barn.

Over the next stile cross the middle of the field to a gated stile and then, keeping this time to the right of a wall, maintain direction to a flight of three steps which climb to yet another gated stile.

Still following the same line, descend a large, open slope to cross Newbiggin Beck and pass through a five-barred gate before swinging right along the foot of Nappa Scar.

About 100 yards before a facing wall take a feint path to the left up through the limestone scar before heading directly across the grass terrace at the top to a gated stile in the wall flanking the Carperby to Askrigg road.

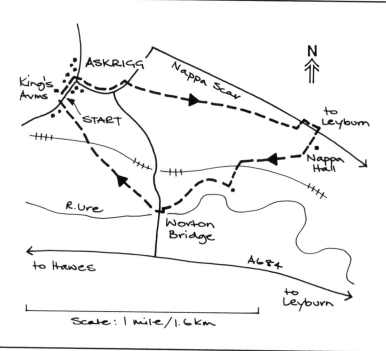

Scale: 1 mile/1.6 km

Turn right along the road for 200 yards before making a right turn into the broad track leading to Nappa Hall which is signed to Worton Bridge.

Nappa Hall, an impressive stone-built castellated building dates from the fourteenth century being built as a fortified farmhouse, perhaps as a defence against the Border Reivers who occasionally penetrated so far south on their cattle stealing forays.

Pass just to the right of the farm and, where the track ends by a footpath sign, turn right through a five-barred gate. Head diagonally left, taking direction from the arm of the footpath finger post and quickly picking up a broad green path.

Through the next five-barred gate head leftwards towards a stone barn by the side of the abandoned railway line. There, stay forward over the railway track onto the driveway to Nappa Mill Farm. At the T-junction in front of the farm, turn right towards a stile with a footpath sign adjacent.

Cross the field to a railed footbridge before turning slightly leftwards to a wall gap with the River Ure close-by on the left. Stay forward to a footbridge, this time by a tree, where the Ure bends away to the left.

Follow the clear riverside path upstream on the right-hand bank to gain the road from Askrigg to Worton, a continuation of Low Lane. Turn left towards Worton Bridge which is some 20 yards away but, by the near-end of the bridge, go through a gate on the right to join a path signed to Askrigg. This soon becomes flagged with fine views up the length of Wensleydale.

After half a mile this path crosses the disused Hawes to Leyburn railway before veering left up the grass embankment to meet a wall on the left at the point where the gradient eases.

Within a short distance pass through a stile to the right of a five-barred gate and immediately turn left along a lane which runs by some fairly new houses.

After 20 yards the track forks. Go left to reach the main road through Askrigg village opposite the parish church. Turn right to regain the King's Arms.

11. CARPERBY

A short, easy walk which visits the most famous waterfalls in the Dales and drops-in at the pub where a Dales author spent his honeymoon.

Route: National Park Information Centre, Aysgarth Falls – Middle Falls – Lower Falls – Hollins House – Low Lane – Carperby – National Park Information Centre.

Distance: 3 miles.

Start: The National Park Information Centre and car park by Aysgarth Falls. Map reference 012887

Map: Ordnance Survey Outdoor Leisure Map number 30, "Yorkshire Dales, Northern and Central Areas".

Public transport: Bus service number 26, Hawes – Leyburn – Richmond stops at Aysgarth Falls. Daily except Sunday. United Bus Company.

Bus service number 159, Hawes – Leyburn – Ripon stops at Carperby. Daily except Sundays. United Bus Company.

Dalesbus service number 800, Harrogate/Leeds – Hawes – Keld calls at Aysgarth Falls. Tuesdays in late July and August and Saturdays and Sundays late July to end of September. Keighley and District Bus Company.

Dalesbus service number 809, Keighley – Richmond, stops at Aysgarth Falls. Tuesdays only in late July and August. Keighley and District Bus Company.

Car: The National Park Information Centre and car park is signed from the A684, Leyburn to Hawes road a short distance east of Aysgarth village. The car park is the converted station yard adjacent to the minor road linking the A684 with Carperby.

THE WHEATSHEAF, CARPERBY

Situated on the main street through the village of Carperby, the Wheatsheaf's chief claim to fame is that James Herriot spent his honeymoon there in 1941. Strangely, for this part of Wensleydale, it has never been used as a location for the filming of the television series, "All Creatures Great and Small".

Although sections of the hotel date back several centuries, the bar is a Victorian addition. Nevertheless, it is snug and cosy, being partially divided into cubicles by wooden panels topped with leaded glass and supported by wooden pillars.

The cushioned wall benches along the walls and the wooden chairs and tables all contribute to the general atmosphere. There are lots of horse brasses, some interesting figures of Robert the Bruce, Henry VIII, Elizabeth I and other historical personages along with a display of plates on a wall shelf.

The drinker has a choice of Webster's Bitter, Webster's Choice and Webster's Pennine, all on hand pump.

Bar snacks are served at lunch time and in the evening while coffee is served from mid-morning.

Opening times: Daily, 12.00 to 15.00 and 18.30 to 23.00. It may stay open longer if custom is thriving.

AYSGARTH FALLS

A short distance to the east of the village of Aysgarth the River Ure flows over three successive limestone steps to form the most famous waterfalls in the Dales. It is a popular spot with day trippers and there is a nature trail through the adjacent woodlands.

Freeholders Wood, nearby, belongs to the local freeholders as the name implies.They still enjoy certain rights such as the collection and gathering of wood.

CARPERBY

Nowadays Carperby is a quiet rural oasis but in bygone centuries it enjoyed the privilege of holding a market centred round the cross which was erected on the village green in 1674. Some splendid examples of lynchets, horizontal strips ploughed along the hillsides, may be seen behind the Wheatsheaf.

THE WALK

Leave the National Park Information Centre, which occupies the converted former railway station, along the path signposted to the Middle and Lower Falls

This parallels the road for a few yards before turning left to cross it to a couple of small wooden gates. 50 yards beyond these turn right down a flight of steps to the viewing platform overlooking the Middle Falls, arguably the most impressive of the three.

The Middle Falls

Retrace your steps to the main path, turning right along it as it continues through Freeholders' Wood which, because of the perpetuating of wood-gathering rights, is heavily coppiced, a practice beneficial for both wildflowers and birds such as robin, chaffinch, chiffchaff, willow warbler and various members of the titmouse family.

At the first junction fork right, following the signs to the Lower Falls. Once again retrace your steps. At the junction turn right onto the path signed to Bolton Castle and Redmire. For a distance this stays just to the right of a wooden fence.

Beyond a gated stile maintain direction over a meadow to meet a rutted track. Turn left along this to Hollins House Farm. Continue between the house and the outbuildings before emerging onto the unsurfaced farm lane which soon makes a large sweep round to the left as it develops into Low Lane.

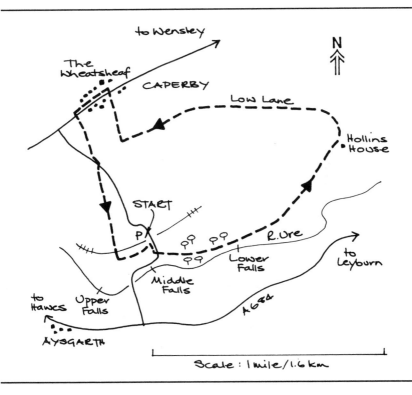

At the first cattle grid ignore two signed paths, one to the right and the other to the left. Stay forwards, crossing more cattle grids and with some extensive views over the middle stretch of Wensleydale.

About a mile from Hollins House, and a little way beyond two new barns on the left, look out for a finger post on the right indicating a path to Carperby village. Opposite is another signed to Aysgarth.

Turn right through the stile and, keeping to the left of a wall, aim for a gateway ahead. Through that veer back towards the wall. A few yards before a facing five-barred gate turn right through a stile and then turn immediately left, thereby maintaining the same line of direction.

Cross a small stream by means of the stepping stones before reaching another five-barred gate which allows passage onto the main road through Carperby opposite the Wheatsheaf.

With thirst quenched, turn right out of the pub to walk through the village as far as the stone market cross which stands on the village green. By the green turn left into the track running through West Grove Farm and which is signed to Aysgarth.

With the farmhouse on the right, advance over two stiles in quick succession before crossing the middle of one field to a gateway and then across a second on a very distinct path to a metal five-barred gate in the far left-hand corner.

This permits access to Low Lane. Turn right for the few yards remaining to the Carperby to Aysgarth road. At the junction turn left. After 20 yards pass through a gated stile which is set into an unusual wall corner on the right.

Stay immediately to the right of a wall but, having negotiated a through stile keep to the right of a row of trees before dropping down a grass slope to cross a rough track. Maintain direction to the right of a clump of trees surrounded by a metal fence.

Eventually a stile alongside a five-barred gate is reached. From there head for the left-hand corner of a fence by a very large tree and, staying to the left of the fence, reach yet another stile.

Beyond, veer slightly to the right through some trees to an old-fashioned metal kissing gate. Go forwards across the bed of the disused railway before descending a flight of steps into the car park by the National Park Information Centre.

To view the Upper Falls follow the signed and waymarked path, retracing your steps to the car park.

12. WEST WITTON

A high level route following a walled lane to the remains of a medieval religious foundation before returning along riverside paths.

Route: West Witton – High Lane – Penhill Preceptory – Scot Gate-Mesnes Plantation – West Witton.

Distance: 5$\frac{1}{4}$ miles.

Start: Wensleydale Heifer Inn, West Witton. Map reference, 063885

Map: Ordnance Survey Outdoor Leisure Map number 30, "Yorkshire Dales, Northern and Central Areas".

Public transport: Bus service number 26, Hawes – Leyburn – Richmond. Daily except Sundays. United Bus Company.

Dalesbus service number 809, Keighley – Skipton – Hawes – Richmond. Fridays, late July and August. Keighley and District Bus Company.

Car: West Witton is situated on the A684 road through Wensleydale about five miles west of Leyburn. There is a lay-by at the eastern approach to the village.

THE WENSLEYDALE HEIFER

The Wensleydale Heifer in West Witton has a comfortable lounge plus two small snug bars, heated in winter by log fires. The snug bars are partially flagged and partially carpeted. The walls are decorated with old sporting prints. It serves bar meals and offers overnight accommodation. Beers served are John Smith's Bitter, Theakston's Bitter and Old Peculier.

Opening times: Monday to Saturday, 11.00 to 23.00; Sunday, 12.00 to 15.00 and 18.00 to 22.30.

WEST WITTON

West Witton was recorded in Domesday Book as "Wittone" meaning "a stone village", but its chief claim to fame lies with the traditional bonfire ceremony which has been held, probably since pre-Christian times, in late August. Known as "Burning of Owd Bartle" or St.Bartholomew, it is held annually on the saint's feast day.

Nearby Pinhill has also been used for centuries as a beacon point. In the past, fires blazed on the hilltop as warnings of approaching danger whereas today they celebrate coronations and jubilees.

PENHILL PRECEPTORY

Penhill Preceptory was built about 1200 as a chapel for the Order of the Knights Templar but was transferred to the Knights Hospitaller in 1320.

The scanty visible remains are of the chapel, excavated in the nineteenth century. The other foundations have never been exposed.

The Wensleydale Heifer

THE WALK

Take the path opposite the Wensleydale Heifer signed to Moor Bank, initially keeping to the right of a stone cottage which now belongs to the pub.

After only a few yards, and by the next footpath sign, go left between stone buildings to follow a winding route flanked by stone walls to a gated stile.

Beyond head diagonally left across the first field to a through stile and then veer left again to negotiate two more before entering a walled lane leading to the minor road linking West Witton with Melmerby.

Turn right along the road, climbing steeply to pass Capple Bank Farm. At the following bend make a right turn into a walled lane signed to Kagram. This can be very wet and muddy after prolonged rain.

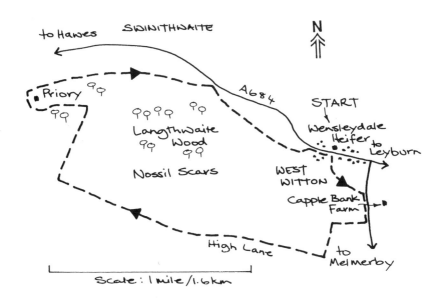

Scale: 1 mile/1.6km

Follow this through a five-barred gate until about 100 yards beyond a derelict barn. There turn left through a squeezer stile onto a distinct path running to the left of a wall to another through stile. Continue in the same direction, climbing steeply again to meet High Lare.

Turn right. As may be imagined from its name, it offers long distance views up Wensleydale as it runs along the contour just below Harrow Ridge and Hunter Thorn.

After a mile a junction is reached. On the left is a footpath signposted to Black Scar, a forbidding hill which is now clearly in view. To the right is a bridleway descending to Nossil End and Langthwaite Lane.

Ignore both. Continue along High Lane for a further half mile to reach a five-barred gate. 200 yards after this, and opposite a ladder stile, turn right into a gated lane. Bolton Castle is prominent directly ahead but, sadly, is located on the far side of the valley.

Where the track bends to the right, the left-hand wall disappears, but the track is easy to distinguish immediately to the left of a wall, Soon it acquires a concrete surface as it commences its steep descent.

It passes a disused quarry where recent tree planting has been carried out. At a footpath sign, indicating a path on the right to Nossill Bank, swing left, still with the concrete track. At the next bend, recognised by two very large stones, go left onto a broad grass track which is unsigned. This veers to the right, soon picking up the boundary wall of a plantation, Langthwaite Wood, before losing height to a five-barred gate. Through that, continue downhill, heading to the right and the obvious fenced-in ruins of Penhill Preceptory.

By the ruins turn sharp right along the path signed to West Witton. This runs to the right of a wall. After half a mile and three stiles it reaches a lane leading to the village of Swinithwaite. Cross directly, go through double gates and maintain direction still with a wall on the left. Another half mile and three more stiles brings the path to a small gate in the wall and a footpath sign.

Ignore the gate which leads onto the main road at Scot Gate. Instead remain along the path signed to West Witton. It swings diagonally right away from the road and across a lush meadow to a through stile. Cross the next field to a prominent five-barred gate before traversing a very large field. Aim first for a telegraph pole and then for the right-hand corner of Mesnes Plantation.

Over a stile continue between a wall on the right and the wood on the left to another stile after 60 yards. Stay to the left of the wall in crossing the subsequent field but, ten yards before a facing wall, turn right to a squeezer stile.

Beyond, turn left immediately to another stile before heading across the centre of the next field to a small gated stile and the A684 on the outskirts of West Witton. Turn right for the village and the Wensleydale Heifer.

13. LEYBURN

A walk along the broad turf path of Leyburn Shawl with some fine views up Wensleydale followed by a mixture of field and riverside paths.

Route: Leyburn – Leyburn Shawl – Tullis Cote – Wensley Park – Wensley – River Ure – Leyburn.

Distance: 7 miles

Start: Leyburn Square. Map reference, 112905.

Map: Ordnance Survey Outdoor Leisure Map number 30, "Yorkshire Dales, Northern and Central Areas".

Public transport: Bus service numbers 26, 158, 178, Richmond to Leyburn. Daily except Sundays. United Bus Company.

Bus service number 159, Hawes – Leyburn – Ripon. Daily except Sundays. United Bus Company.

Bus service numbers 73, 178, Leyburn – Bedale – Northallerton. Daily except Sundays. Connects with British Rail main line services from London and Scotland at Northallerton. United Bus Company.

Dalesbus service number 803, Leeds – Harrogate – Ripon – Leyburn – Hawes Summer Sundays only. Harrogate and District Bus Company.

Car: Leyburn is situated on the A6108 Ripon to Richmond road, the A684, Leyburn to Northallerton road which intersects the A1 at Leeming Bar. From Leyburn the A684 continues through Wensleydale to Hawes and Sedbergh to Kendal.

There is parking on the market square and also in a nearby car park.

THE SANDPIPER

The unusually-named Sandpiper is to be found near the bottom end of the Market Square in Leyburn, a quiet oasis sufficiently removed from the main hustle and bustle of the town centre. It is little more than a small, attractive stone cottage festooned on the outside with cotoneaster, honeysuckle and climbing roses. During the summer months the front terrace is laid out with white cast-iron tables.

Including the back room, reached by three steps, there are only seven tables in the low-ceilinged, beamed bar. The walls are decorated with photographs of the Dales, toby jugs and Delft ware including a collection of teapots.

Near the servery is a collection of stuffed sandpipers, more photographs and a woodburning stove set into the stone fireplace. There is a small, separate dining area for a range of bar snacks and more substantial dishes. There is no food on winter Mondays. For the drinker there is Theakston's Best and Webster's Yorkshire Bitter on handpump with Ruddles Best Bitter as an additional choice.

Opening times: Monday to Thursday, 11.00 to 14.30 and 18.30 to 23.00; Friday and Saturday, 11.00 to 15.00 and 18.30 to 23.00; Sunday, 11.00 to 14.30; Closed Sunday evenings and all day Monday during the winter.

The Sandpiper

LEYBURN

Shortly after 1066 the new French owner of this part of Wensleydale, lands given to him by William the Conqueror for services rendered during the invasion, named Leyburn after his native Libourne in southern France, and laid out the village along the same lines.

Despite this it remained comparatively obscure until it developed as a staging centre during the Turnpike era. Its importance is based on its strategic position on the A684, Northallerton to Kendal road which is one of the main trans-Pennine routes. It also sits on the junction with the 6108.

The initial boost to its prosperity resulted from the grant of a market charter in 1684 during the reign of Charles II, making it the commercial centre for Lower Wensleydale.Many of the buildings date only from the start of the nineteenth century.

SHAWL TERRACE

A narrow road from the top of the Market Square leads to Shawl Terrace, a wide, grassy escarpment which offers some long range views up Wensleydale. One point is known as "Queen's Gap" because, according to tradition, Mary Queen of Scots was recaptured there after escaping from nearby Bolton Castle during her imprisonment in the reign of Elizabeth I.

The discovery of several rubbing stones for grinding corn, along with other prehistoric cooking implements, suggests that until the Norman Conquest, this is where the early settlers made their homes.

The origin of this curious name is Scandinavian. It is derived from the Norse word, "Scale" or "Skali" which is usually translated as the "huts of settlers", similar to Scottish "Shealing".

BOLTON PARK

Although Bolton Hall is closed to the public several rights of way cross the beautiful parkland. The Hall was built in 1678 to replace Bolton Castle which had suffered extensively during the Civil War.

WENSLEY

The attractive village of Wensley, set around its green, is the only village in the National Park to give its name to the dale.Until the plague of 1563 decimated its population, it was the most important market centre in the dale. It never recovered.

Its ancient water mill, close by the bridge, is now used as a pottery while the parish church was fortunate to escape the great rebuilding mania of the nineteenth century.

Most of the structure dates from the thirteenth and fifteenth centuries with a delicately carved wooden screen from Easby Abbey, the Bolton box pew and an unusual reliquary near the door. The most notable grave in the churchyard is that of Peter Goldsmith a surgeon who attended Nelson after his fatal wound on HMS Victory.

Wensley Church

THE WALK

From the market square cross the A6108 into a much smaller square and exit by the far right hand corner following a sign "To the Shawl". After a few yards pass through an old-fashioned metal kissing gate onto a flagged path which soon gives way to a broad, grassy swathe. There is a football ground and a children's playground on the right with the main road through Wensleydale, the A684, below on the left.

More distantly the bulk of Capple Bank and the length of Wensleydale offer an enticing perspective for further exploration. The only blight is Moor Quarry which lies to the right. The broad path climbs gently along the edge of the limestone escarpment known as Leyburn Shawl, a favourite promenade for the local residents. After three squeezer stiles in succession, the path runs just inside some woodlands, emerging from time to time to provide stunning views.

Beyond a fourth stile adjacent to two concrete gateposts there is a junction. Fork right to a waymarked stile 15 yards ahead. Moor Quarry has been left behind and the village of Wensley nestles in the valley on the left. Continue with the path through Warren Wood until it swings sharply left for a few yards to a stile. Beyond, turn sharp left through a stile in a derelict wall, before maintaining direction down the sloping field to a rickety stile by a hawthorn tree.

By this turn right, as waymarked, heading diagonally right across a field towards a large, blue metal gate. Through this turn right along a broad track but, after 100 yards and by the end of a rocky outcrop where the track arcs left, continue forward on a less distinct path in the direction of Gill Field Wood. This soon meets another broad track running downhill immediately outside the woodland boundary.

Turn left to Tullis Cote, the word "Cote" indicating a shelter for sheep and other animals. By the last building of Tullis Cote Farm maintain direction by taking the right-hand fork. At the subsequent junction turn right to emerge onto the minor road leading to Preston-under-Scar.

Cross directly to a field path which goes over the railway (now carrying only mineral traffic) and another field to the minor road to Redmire.

Turn left along this for 150 yards and then right onto a broad track, as signed, to enter the woodlands of Bolton Hall. Thirty yards into the

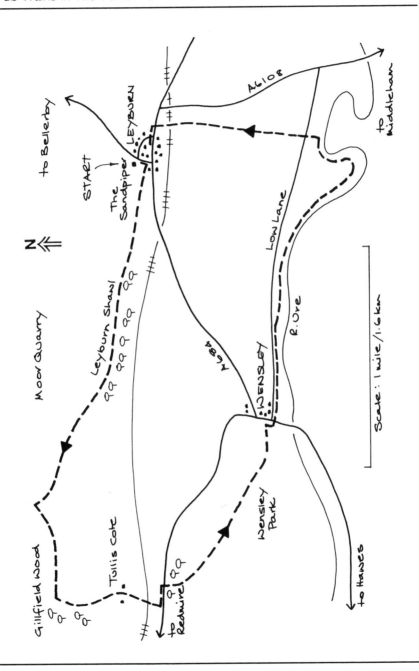

woods turn sharp left onto a narrower path leading to a five-barred gate complete with waymarker sign.

Leave the woods through this, initially turn right to follow the field boundary, having a wall and the woods on the right. Pass through another large waymarked gate on the right and stay forward to the left of a fence. Where this corners away to the right, maintain direction over the open parkland, passing between a solitary tree on the left and some pheasant breeding pens on the right.

This is Wensley Park which belongs to Bolton Hall. Beyond the pens the indistinct path heads for a second solitary tree before aiming for the right-hand corner of another plantation and a large metal gate. Turn left along the driveway. After a quarter of a mile the village green in the centre of Wensley village is reached.

Turn right onto the A684 and, after 20 yards, left into Low Lane, a minor road leading to Middleham. Stay along this for approximately half a mile. By an unofficial lay-by on the right, turn through a metal gate to join a well-trodden riverside path alongside the Ure. Negotiate three stiles in succession before staying with the river as it forms a large loop to the south and then changes direction to the north.

But, where it swings eastwards again, continue forward up a small facing bank to a stile. Veer right across the field to a five-barred gate in the far corner. This affords access to Low Lane. Cross directly onto a signed footpath which at first passes to the right of a plantation.

Over the first stile avoid the temptation to take the more obvious path heading diagonally to the right. Instead, take a less obvious but still distinct path which stays to the right of the plantation until it picks up a fence on the left.

Follow this round to a stile set into a short stretch of facing wall. Proceed up the narrow field to a squeezer stile alongside a gate. Maintain direction up the next field to a gate and then to a stile which is followed, after ten yards, by a cattle grid. At this point turn right along the road which rounds a new housing estate. After ten yards, go left along a grass path between the houses. Avoid all side turnings to reach a short flight of steps.

At the top turn left over the railway bridge and keep forward to the A684. Go left along this to reach the market square and the Sandpiper.

14. MIDDLEHAM

This moderate route through one of the lesser-known dales visits a castle and abbey before returning over one of the most famous horse-training grounds in the country.

Route: Middleham – Hullo Bridge – Coverham Abbey – Fern Gill – Middleham Low Moor – Middleham

Distance: 6$^1/_2$ miles.

Start: Black Swan Hotel, Middleham.

Map: Ordnance Survey Outdoor Leisure Map number 30, "Yorkshire Dales, Northern and Central Areas".

Public transport: Bus service 159, Hawes – Leyburn – Ripon. Daily except Sundays. United Bus Company.

Bus service number 160, Leyburn – Thornton Steward. Fridays only. United Bus Company.

Bus service 158, Leyburn-Woodale. Fridays only. United Bus Company.

Dalesbus service number 803, Leeds – Harrogate – Ripon – Leyburn – Reeth – Hawes. Summer Sundays and Bank Holidays only. Harrogate and District Bus Company.

Car: Middleham lies on the A6108 road between Ripon and Richmond. It may also be approached from Kettlewell by the minor road through Coverdale. There is limited parking in the market square.

THE BLACK SWAN, MIDDLEHAM

The elegant Georgian facade of the Black Swan fronts onto Middleham's ancient cobbled Market Square. The attractive south facing beer garden at the rear backs onto the castle which is floodlit every evening throughout the summer. It may incorporate stone from the castle but for the most part it dates from the eighteenth century and is a Grade II Listed Building.

The bar, which is on two levels, has a beamed ceiling, bare stone walls decorated with racing prints and poems and built-in highbacked wooden settles. There is also a large stone fireplace with a welcoming blaze in winter. The excellent and extensive bar menu is couched in racing terms and there is en-suite overnight accommodation.

Beers served are Theakston's Bitter, XB and Old Peculier.

Opening times: Daily, 11.00 to 15.00 and 16.00 to 23.00; Sunday, 12.00 to 15.00 and 19.00 to 22.30.

MIDDLEHAM

Middleham is the racehorse training capital of the North with several hundred thoroughbreds divided between five stables in the town and a further six in the immediate neighbourhood. Every morning, winter and summer, the sound of hooves on cobbles echoes through the town as the horses head out to Low Moor for their daily gallops.

The town itself, two miles south of Leyburn, nestles beneath the substantial and imposing remains of the Norman Castle. The first, constructed shortly after the Conquest on William's Hill, was replaced in 1170.

The Castle, Middleham

In 1472 it passed into the ownership of the Duke of Gloucester, later to become Richard III, through his marriage to Anne Neville, daughter of the Earl of Warwick, "The Kingmaker". The future monarch and his wife made Middleham their home throughout the later stages of the War of the Roses, leaving only when he was crowned king in 1483. Today it is maintained by English Heritage.

Charles Kingsley, author of "The Water Babies", was the last canon of St. Alkeda's Church, a Collegiate foundation dating from the fifteenth century. It is named after a Saxon princess martyred by the Danes for refusing to renounce her Christian faith.

Middleham's right to a market was granted in the fourteenth century and confirmed in 1479 by Richard III, an event marked by the Swine Cross which stands in the Market Place. The square is surrounded by Georgian houses and hotels, testifying to the town's importance throughout the coaching era.

COVERHAM ABBEY

Founded at Swainby in 1195, this abbey of Premonstratensian monks transferred to its present site in Coverdale in 1212, remaining there until the Dissolution of the Monasteries. Along with their counterparts of nearby Jervaulx, the monks of Coverham are credited with introducing horse racing to the Middleham area as well as producing the first Coverdale cheese.

Little now remains of the abbey which has passed into private ownership. However, this walk goes through the gatehouse from where there is a good view of the monastic guesthouse which has been incorporated into a later dwelling.

The monks were responsible for serving the nearby parish church of Holy Trinity. This, too, dates from the thirteenth century although it has undergone extensive alterations and modification throughout the intervening centuries.

A declining population forced services to end in 1986 and it is maintained by the Redundant Churches Fund. It has a simple interior with a beamed roof and some stained glass and a Saxon carving over the doorway.

THE WALK

From the Black Swan walk up the road for a few yards before turning into the cobbled lane to the left of the Castle Tea Room. Continue along the lane with the castle on the right, to pass through a five-barred gate for the start of a gradual climb to the left of a wall.

Away to the right, on the crest of William's Hill, are the remains of the Motte and Bailey of the original Middleham Castle.

At the top of the rise pause briefly to admire the views before losing height to reach a stile. Maintain the line of direction but with a wall now on the left.

Where the path commences its final, sharp dip towards the banks of the River Cover, swing right, as indicated by a waymarker fastened to a tree. On the left is the boundary fence of a wood.

By some barns, and 20 yards before a facing five-barred gate, go over a stile on the left. Keeping to the right of the fence, follow round the perimeter of the field until the path veers to the left and widens into a track descending through some trees to the river bank.

Soon a stile is reached alongside Hullo Bridge, a stone arched affair spanning the Cover. Do not cross. Instead continue forward along the broad green track which, after a few yards, arcs to the right before climbing up the large field to pass through a five-barred gate onto the minor road which runs through Coverdale from Middleham.

Turn left along the road to enter the Yorkshire Dales National Park. Five yards beyond this boundary go through a gate on the left. Ignoring the upper path signed to Coverham Abbey, stay to the left of the wall, losing height rapidly back to the bank of the river.

Swing right by another waymarker fixed to a tree to pass some barns where the path widens into a lane. Beyond a stile and another five-barred gate it reverts to a narrow path running along the right-hand boundary of a field to a gate.

Through that it changes back into a lane to pass to the right of a building with a corrugated roof and, shortly afterwards, some of the remains of Coverham Abbey.

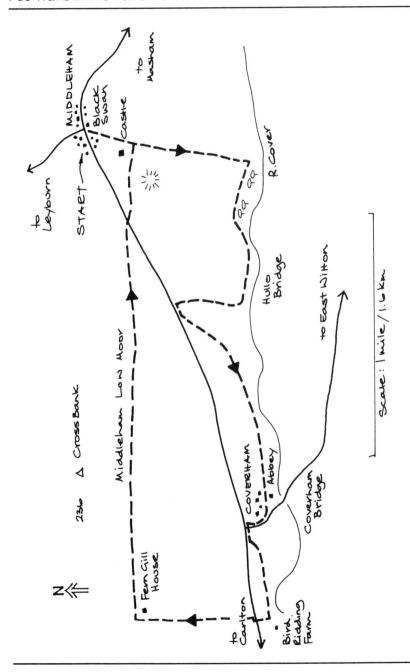

Cross an intersecting lane to pass Coverdale Nursery on the right and then beneath the arch of the medieval gateway of the abbey to meet Hanghow Lane. To obtain a view of Coverdale Bridge go left for a few yards, otherwise turn right along the surfaced road to gain the main Coverdale road from Middleham to Kettlewell. Holy Trinity Church, well worth a visit, is on the right.

Turn left along the road but, after 200 yards, turn left onto the path signed to Bird Ridding Farm. This crosses a couple of fields to the farm driveway.

Turn right along this regaining the main road through an impressive gateway. This time turn right onto the road but, after 40 yards go left through an even more impressive gateway to walk up a wide, metalled drive which gives the impression of leading to a stately home.

Do not be overawed. Despite appearances and the complete absence of all signs at this point, it is a public right of way. At the first Y-junction, fork right in the direction of West Park. At the subsequent intersection continue forward through the gates of Ferngill House on an unmetalled bridleway pock-marked with horses' hooves.

Stay to the left of the house itself to a tall, narrow metal gate set into a well-preserved drystone wall. On the far side turn right immediately onto the wide grassy track as it gradually veers away from the wall to parallel, originally, some overhead wires. This is Middleham Low Moor, used extensively for the daily gallops of the area's racehorses. During the morning it is wise to keep eyes and ears open.

The path stays to the left of the Triangulation Pillar at 236 metres on the crest of Cross Bank. From this vast, open expanse there are extensive views reaching as far as the North Yorkshire Moors on a clear day.

After almost two miles the bridleway joins the main Coverdale road. Cross almost directly to a signed path which initially runs for some distance to the right of the wall separating it from the road. At the first stile it goes right to pass behind Middleham Castle to meet the outward route. Turn left into the town centre.

15. CARLTON

A short, moderate walk through undulating countryside in Coverdale with a short stretch of open moorland.

Route: Carlton – Howden Gill – Gammersgill – Turn Beck – Carlton Moor – Carlton.

Distance: 4 miles.

Start: Foresters' Arms, Carlton, Coverdale. Map reference, 066847

Map: Ordnance Survey Outdoor Leisure Map number 30, "Yorkshire Dales, Northern and Central Areas."

Public transport: Bus service number 158, Leyburn – Woodale, Fridays only. United Bus Company.

Car: Carlton is on the minor, unclassified road from Middleham through Coverdale to Kettlewell, about five miles south west of Middleham. Parking, for patrons only, at the Foresters' Arms. It is also possible to find roadside parking in the village.

THE FORESTERS' ARMS, CARLTON

The Foresters' Arms is a small pub with a great atmosphere. It has two small but cosy bars with flagged floors and open fires. The windows command some outstanding views of the local fells.

The bar walls are lined with sporting cartoons plus a photograph of the Coverdale Friendly Society wearing uniform and regalia, taken outside the pub in 1989. There is also a nineteenth century certificate of the Ancient Order of Foresters.

The Foresters was once a changing stage for the horses hauling the coaches on the London to Richmond stage.

Beers are Smith's Bitter and Bayhouse along with Theakston's XB and Bitter. Bar meals are also served.

Opening times: Monday to Saturday, 12.00 to 15.00 and 19.00 to 23.00; Sunday, 12.00 to 15.00 and 19.00 to 22.30.

The Home of Henry Constantine, "The Bard of Coverdale"

CARLTON

Carlton, an attractive village strung-out along the main road through Coverdale, was part of the royal hunting forest owned by the Lords of Middleham during medieval times, although little evidence of this still remains on the ground. Later, deposits of coal and lead were worked extensively on Carlton Moor. To serve these during the eighteenth and nineteenth centuries a network of bridleways and packhorse routes was developed. Today many of these provide excellent routes for the walker.

Coverdale was also noted for the high quality of the flagstones it produced from the quarries whose remains still litter the hillsides and slopes above Carlton.

One sign of the village's former importance and wealth is the large number of sturdy, stone-built yeomens' houses which also date from the eighteenth and nineteenth centuries. One has an inscription above its doorway commemorating Henry Constantine, a dialect poet known as the Bard of Coverdale. He lived there until his death in 1807.

THE WALK

Start by walking along the road through the village towards Kettlewell. 200 yards from the Forresters' Arms, and just by the Post Office, fork left over a stream to pass to the right of a row of cottages. There is a footpath sign pointing to Flats Hill at a distance of 250 yards.

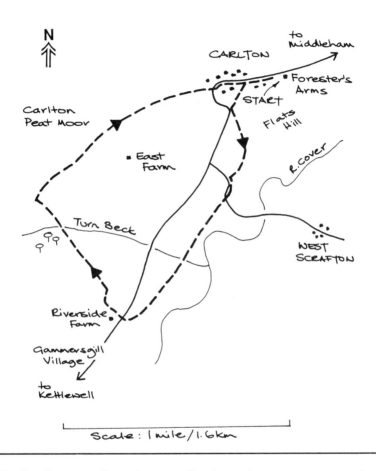

By the final cottage, go through a small gate and across a succession of five small fields using a series of squeezer stiles to the road at Flats Hill.

Turn left. Immediately go through a five-barred gate on the left to follow another path signed to Cover Lane. Descend down the centre of the field to a step stile some 20 yards to the left of a facing gate and then turn diagonally right to a through stile. Stay to the right of a wall to another which permits access to the road heading for West Scrafton.

Turn left but after 100 yards and where the road arcs sharply to the left, climb the rather obscure stile on the right which has another footpath sign adjacent. Keep to the right of the fence. After 20 yards, and another stile, there is a wall on the left until another through stile is reached.

From there, stay to the left of a fence, drop to cross a stream and then proceed along a grass terrace, aiming slightly to the left of a red gate. Do not pass through the gate. Instead advance between some trees on the left and a fence on the right to a gateway only a few yards further on than the red gate. Through this gateway cross an open field, heading for a wall corner and keeping to the right of a wall to a small gate. Cross the next field and a small footbridge to another gate affording access to Turnbeck Lane.

This is rapidly becoming overgrown, the walker having to bend double to pass beneath large trees felled by repeated gales. Turnbeck Lane leads to a through stile beyond which traverse the following field rightwards to meet the road by the entrance to Gammersgill village.

Turn left but, almost at once and before the first house, go right onto a field path signed to Fleensop, one of the former colliery workings on Carlton Moor. Stay to the right of the house, cross open ground to a wall on the left and eventually reach a five-barred gate. Go through this, but turn right immediately, following the waymarks around the inside of the field boundary before making a right turn through another five-barred gate. Keep forward but, after only a short distance, swing left, as waymarked, to cross Turn Beck.

On the far bank turn left, heading upstream before swinging round to the right and climbing steeply for some distance to a through stile. Maintain direction to the left of a derelict stone barn and then turn left through a gateway. Immediately make a sharp right turn and, staying to the left of a wall, advance to another five-barred gate. Through this turn right. Keep to the left of a wall, pass through yet another five-barred gate and over a cattle grid.

From this point the path develops into a bridleway as it passes to the left of East Farm, and meets another bridleway on a right-angled bend. Go forward. The track quickly acquires a metalled surface to become a road heading into Carlton. At the main road turn left to regain the Foresters' Arms.

16. HORSEHOUSE

A high level moorland walk offering some unusual views of Great Whernside.

Route: Horsehouse – Well House – Hindlethwaite Grange – Swineside – Arkleside Pasture – Stone Road – Arkleside – Horsehouse.

Distance: 7 miles.

Start: Thwaite Arms, Horsehouse, Coverdale. Map reference 047814

Map: Ordnance Survey Outdoor Leisure Map number 30, "Yorkshire Dales, Northern and Central Areas."

Public transport: Bus service number 158, Leyburn – Woodale. Fridays only, United Bus Company.

Car: Horsehouse is located on the main road through Coverdale from Middleham to Kettlewell. There is a car park for patrons only at the Thwaite Arms and a limited amount of roadside parking in the village.

THE THWAITE ARMS, HORSEHOUSE

This low-roofed, stone-built pub is located in the centre of the tiny village of Horsehouse, almost opposite the church. The bar is tiny, with only four tables. Seating is provided mainly on cushioned settles lining the walls, with the addition of some bar stools. The bottom of the walls is wainscoted, the upper half cream-coloured. They are decorated with climbing and mountaineering photographs.

The ceiling is beamed. In winter there is a roaring log fire while in summer there are tables and benches outside. There is also a slightly larger side bar and a dining room. Tony and Doreen Longstaff offer a warm welcome to walkers who have discovered the delights of Coverdale, which are many. Despite its comparative remoteness the Thwaite Arms offers John Smith's Bitter, Theakston's Bitter, XB, and Old Peculier, all on hand pump. There is also a tempting range of bar meals which alters according to the weather.

Opening times: Monday to Friday, 19.00 to 23.00; Saturday, 12.00 to 15.00 and 19.00 to 23.00; Sunday, 12.00 to 15.00 and 19.00 to 22.30.

HORSEHOUSE

Horsehouse was situated at the junction of several packhorse routes. One traversed the wild moorlands at the head of Coverdale to Kettlewell, more or less following the line of the present road. Others crossed from Nidderdale and from Wensleydale. Some were of local significance, linking the valley floor with the coal and lead mines on Fleensop and Carlton moors.

The Thwaite Arms was once a coaching inn on the London to Richmond road. Either after or before the long, steep haul over Hunters Sleets a change of horses was required. This change was affected in the village, a practice which gave rise to the name, Horsehouse.

Horsehouse Church

THE WALK

From the Thwaite Arms take the road towards Middleham. After 330 yards, and opposite Well House, turn right into the broad track which soon crosses the River Cover by a delightful stone bridge before swinging right to head towards Hindlethwaite Grange.

A little way before a five-barred gate turn left over a stile onto a path to Swineside. Climb a second stile after 15 yards before immediately turning left through another five-barred gate.

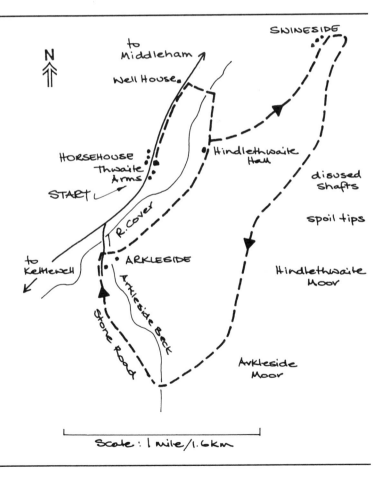

Scale: 1 mile/1.6km

Almost at once join a broad track running uphill. Where this track makes a 90 degree turn to the right, after some 300 yards, make another left turn onto a narrower but clear path over the rough moorland.

Beyond the next stile head right to a small gate before turning left through 45 degrees to a squeezer stile which is hard to spot. Beyond, continue the climb up the flank of Rampshaw Bank until the gradient eases to offer superb views both up and down Coverdale.

On the far side of a wall gap continue along the widening path through more gateways to a five-barred gate with a stile and footpath sign alongside. Stay forward to the right of a row of cottages which constitute the tiny hamlet of Swineside.

Reaching the road turn right. Within 150 yards go right onto the bridleway signed to Arkleside Pasture. This maintains a fairly straight line but quickly narrows as it traverses the high moors separating Coverdale from Nidderdale.

It continues for two miles with Little and Great Whernside directly ahead in the far distance. It swings left into Hindlethwaite Gill, crosses the beck, and heads out again before veering to the left of a large patch of reeds. There is a parallel stone wall some distance to the right.

A little way below High Crag it reaches a stile in a facing wire fence. Over that stay forward to a small metal gate, followed by a wooden one before a sharp, short drop to cross Arkelside Beck. Climb the far bank to another small wooden gate by the side of a rough bridleway. With Dead Man's Hill conspicuous to the left, turn right onto the bridleway known locally as "The Stone Road."

Descend this for about a mile into the minuscule hamlet of Arkleside. Notice the lintel of one house carrying the date of 1627 and the initials on either side, "TH" and "IH".

The track acquires a surface as it passes through Arkleside and continues alongside the River Cover before turning left over a stone bridge to the main valley road.

However, do not cross the bridge. Where the track swings left, turn right along another broad track leading to Soursett Farm. A short distance before the farm, and by a footpath finger post, turn left onto the signed path across a meadow.

Beyond the first small gate continue forward to meet yet another track. Turn right along this as it climbs before making a left turn to pass above a plantation to a ladder stile.

Stay forward to the left of a fence with Horsehouse Moor above to the right. Through a wall gap the path becomes more distinct. At the next footpath sign ignore the arrow. Instead turn left onto the track leading to a five-barred gate.Pass through that, and a second, to re-join the outward route back into Horsehouse and a welcome pint at the Thwaite Arms.

17. YOCKENTHWAITE

A high level outward route provides excellent views across Upper Wharfedale in the heart of the Yorkshire Dales National Park. The return is a gentle stroll along riverside paths.

Route: Hubberholme – Scar House – Yockenthwaite – Hubberholme.

Distance: $3^{1}/_{2}$ miles

Start: George Inn, Hubberholme, Upper Wharfedale. Map reference 925782

Map: Ordnance Survey Outdoor Leisure Map number 30, "Yorkshire Dales, Northern and Central Areas".

Public transport: There is no public transport to Hubberholme but there is a regular year-round bus service from Skipton to Buckden about a mile away. See Cray walk for details.

Car: Follow the B6160 north from Skipton to Buckden. There, fork left as signposted along the minor road which runs through Hubberholme to Hawes. Pub car park and roadside parking.

THE GEORGE, HUBBERHOLME

John Frederick Foster and his wife Marjorie are accustomed to ramblers calling in for a pint at all seasons of the year because The George is deservedly the best known of all the pubs in the Dales. A great favourite with the Bradford author, J.B. Priestly, it stands on the opposite side of the bridge to the equally famous church.

It is located by a beautiful stretch of the River Wharfe and cradled on all sides by rolling moorlands. Originally it was the vicarage, remaining church property until 1964.

This link is perpetuated every New Year's Day by the ancient ritual of "letting the Poor Pasture", when local farmers bid for the tenancy of a field behind the pub. The profits are still used to assist poor people in the parish.

The George epitomises all that a good walker's pub should be. There are two small flagstoned bars, bare stone walls and a dark wooden ceiling supported by massive beams. The copper-topped tables are surrounded by cushioned seats and in winter a cheerful log fire is kept burning in the large fireplace.

The entrance, with a coat of arms over the portico, is round the back or is it that the George was originally built with its back to the road?

Enormous helpings of food may be washed down with a choice from Younger's Scotch or Younger's Number 3, both on handpump. For anyone looking for something stronger there's a selection of 20 malt whiskies.

Opening times: Monday to Thursday, 11.30 to 14.30 and 19.00 to 23.00; Friday, 11.30 to 14.30 and 18.30 to 23.00; Saturday, 11.30 to 15.00 and 18.30 to 23.00; Sunday, 12.00 to 15.00 and 19.00 to 22.30.

ST. MICHAEL'S AND ALL ANGELS

St. Michael's and All Angels Church at Hubberholme stands in an idyllic setting by the River Wharfe with sweeping moorlands rising in all directions. It attracts visitors from all four corners of the world.

Church of St. Michael and All Angels

Originally it was a forest chapel in the days when Langstrothdale Chase was a royal hunting ground rich in deer and other game. It is thought to have been erected on the site of an Anglo-Norse burial ground, the earliest known written mention dating back to 1214. In fact the present Lady Chapel may have been the original chapel.

Its rood loft is one of only two still surviving in Yorkshire, having been transferred from Coverham Priory in 1558, shortly after the Dissolution of the Monasteries.

There are two bells hanging in the tower. They are of modern origin, having been made in 1904 when they replaced a larger cracked one which was cast in 1602. Now standing on the floor of the nave this carries the coat-of-arms of Queen Elizabeth I along with the words, "Jesus be my speed". There is also a memorial to J.B. Priestley who was a frequent visitor and whose ashes were scattered nearby.

The choir stalls and pews are carved with mice, the trademark of the famous Thompson of Kilburn who made them in 1934.

ENCLOSURES

Beyond Buckden Wharfedale changes its name to Langstrothdale, a famous medieval hunting ground. Today's landscape shows ample evidence of the enclosure movement of the late eighteenth and early nineteenth centuries when the bare, open hillside and lower pastures were divided into rectangular fields by hundreds of miles of drystone walls.

Originally the area had been settled by small Norse farming communities who have left their imprint in such names as Yockenthwaite. After the Norman Conquest much of the land passed into the possession of Bolton and Fountains Abbeys for use as extensive sheep granges. It was the monks who created the network of green lanes which traverse the district.

THE WALK

From the George cross the road bridge before passing to the right of the Church of St. Oswald and All Angels and then turning left through a five-barred gate. Proceed to a path junction by the far corner of the church.

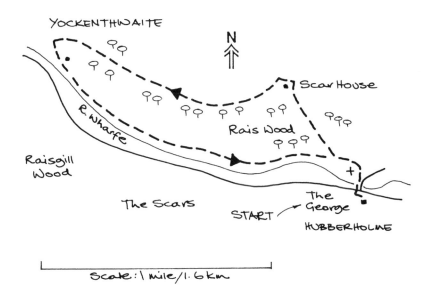

Fork right up the broad track signed to Scar House. After climbing steeply for some distance continue between the farm buildings to a T-junction with a footpath finger post.

Turn left in the direction of Yockenthwaite, following the broad stoney track in a semi-circle to the left before reaching a stone step stile adjacent to a five-barred gate.

Over this the path keeps to the left of some trees, crossing some exposed patches of limestone pavement and offering good quality high level walking accompanied by extensive vistas of Langstrothdale Chase. Kirk Gill Moor and Horsehead Moor are to the left, beyond the River Wharfe which flows down through the valley below. On reaching a gated stile pass through to enter a corner of Rakes Wood, now owned by the National Trust and consisting principally of broad-leaved trees with a scattering of Scots Pines.

Leave the wood by a footbridge with a stile at either end and turn left to a stone step stile. Cross more limestone scars and outcrops to another stile and then a third. Beyond this the route is waymarked but navigational care is needed. After passing to the left of a stone barn, perched a little way above on the hillside, keep a sharp eye open for a yellow arrow painted low down on a broken wall on the left. There, turn left, losing height as the path drops down the slope.

On reaching a facing wall turn right as signed, staying with the contour on a scrubby hillside until meeting a stoney track. Turn left for the sharp descent into the scattered hamlet of Yockenthwaite with both the river and the road snaking up the valley towards Beckermonds.

By Top Farm in Yockenthwaite turn left at a T-junction onto the Dales Way. Proceed in front of the farmhouse, pass through a gateway and stay forward for 20 yards to a gated stile. Through that turn right to a through stile and then sharp left onto the riverside path which has the Wharfe to the right.

This is an interesting stretch because the river alternates between stretches where it flows rapidly over the shallow stoney bed or lies in languid pools where trout bask in sunny weather.

Stay alongside the river and pass through a series of stiles until, a little way beyond a barn, the path appears blocked by a wire fence. Turn left through a small metal gate and then, after a further ten yards, turn right through a gateway and head for a waymarked gap.

Along this section observe the unusual terracing on the lower slopes of Horse Head and Kirk Gill moors to the right, especially by Raisgill Wood. This has been created by layered limestone outcrops.

After crossing a wooden footbridge aim for a waymarked stile some 25 yards to the left of a five-barred gate. Then stay alongside the Wharfe until the square, squat tower of Hubberholme church comes into view.

Keep to the left of the church to a signpost, turn right to a gate and then cross the old stone bridge over the river to return to the George.

18. CRAY

This walk, which is based on three pubs, involves a stiff climb which is rewarded by breathtaking views unrivalled in the National Park.

Route: Buckden – Rakes Wood – Buckden Rake – Cray – Stubbing Bridge – Hubberholme – Buckden

Distance: 5 miles.

Start: National Park car park at the northern end of Buckden village. Map reference 943773

Map: Ordnance Survey Outdoor Leisure Map number 30, "Yorkshire Dales, Northern and Central Areas".

Public transport: Bus service number 72, Skipton – Buckden. Daily except winter Sundays. Keighley and District Bus Company.

Dalesbus service number 800, Harrogate/Leeds – Hawes. Summer Tuesdays, Saturdays and Sundays. Keighley and District Bus Company.

Dalesbus service number 809, Keighley – Richmond. Tuesdays and Fridays in late July and August. Keighley and District Bus Company.

Car: Buckden is situated on the B6160, about 19 miles north of Skipton. There is a large National Park car park at the northern end of the village.

THE WHITE LION, CRAY

Walkers especially are accorded a warm welcome by Frank and Barbara Hardy if they choose to call at the White Lion in the hamlet of Cray. Nestling beneath Buckden Pike at the head of Wharfedale, this sturdy stone pub is the highest in the valley at 1,100 feet above sea level.

Its flagged, uncarpetted floor is typical of the area. In winter there is always a cheery log fire while in summer there are tables and benches outside by Cray Beck.

It has a creamy coloured wooden ceiling with beams and suspended chamber pots, a cushioned settle alongside one of the bare walls of the bar and a scattering of tables and chairs.

The White Lion prides itself on its hand-drawn ales which include Moorhouse's Premier, Moorhouse's Pendle Witches' Brew, Younger's Bitter and Theakston's Bitter.

Bar food is available at lunch time and in the evenings and there is also some en-suite accommodation for anyone wishing to spend a few days exploring the surroundings hills.

Opening times: 11.00 to 23.00.

THE BUCK, BUCKDEN

Located close to the beginning of this walk, the Buck has recently had its bar converted into an open-plan design. Local pictures, hunting scenes and willow-patterned plates adorn the walls. Not surprisingly there is a roe buck's head. The built-in wall benches are upholstered and the tables a highly polished brown.

The Buck Inn

The Buck's bar is now carpeted although the snug area retains its flags and there is a log fire in the colder weather. Seating on the terrace and by the large sycamore tree affords good views of the surrounding countryside when the weather is clear.

Drinkers have a choice between John Smith's Bitter, Tetley's Bitter, Theakston's Old Peculier and a guest beer. As with most other pubs bar meals are served at lunch time and in the evenings and there is overnight accommodation.

Opening times: 11.00 to 23.00

The third pub encountered on this short walk is the George at Hubberholme (see Yockenthwaite walk).

THE WALK

Pass through the gate at the northern end of the car park to begin the long gradual ascent of the bridleway signed to Buckden Pike and Cray High Bridge. This follows the line of the Bainbridge to Ilkley Roman road as it climbs through the scattered remnants of a woodland. Sections of the surface appear to have been paved with sets at sometime in the past but the main surface is composed of the underlying limestone.

For much of the way the route is unfenced but 100 yards before the first five-barred gate acquires a wall on the left. Once through the gate the gradient eases, the countryside becoming far more open with views of Upper Wharfedale and Langstrothdale Chase which make the initial climb worthwhile.

By a second five-barred gate there is a junction. A signed path to Buckden Pike strikes out to the right. Ignore this, keeping forward through the gate. The broad, well-defined path stays just to the right of the wall. The surface has been transformed into excellent springy turf which makes for relaxing walking.

A third gate is easily recognised by the massive limestone boulder that has been utilised as a gatepost. Beyond, the wall on the left disappears, so maintain the line of direction to a stile from where the wall is picked up once again.

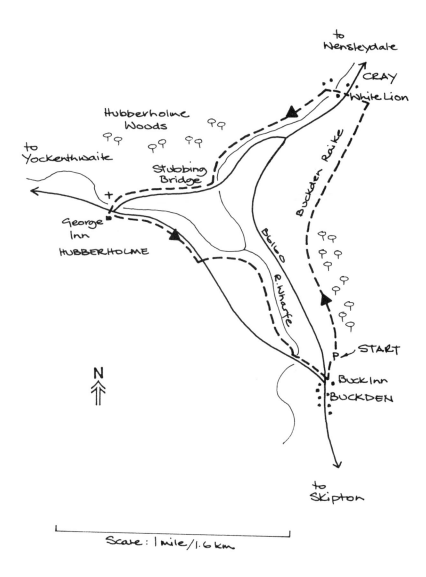

to
Wensleydale

CRAY

White Lion

Buckden Rake

Hubberholme
Woods

to
Yockenthwaite

Stubbing
Bridge

George
Inn
HUBBERHOLME

R. Wharfe

P — START

Buck Inn
BUCKDEN

N

to
Skipton

Scale: 1 mile/1.6 km

75 yards beyond the stile turn left through a small gate onto a narrower but still distinct path which drops down the slope to meet a wall on the right. Remain to the left of this but, by a wall corner with a footpath sign adjacent, turn right.

Continue the descent, finally fording Cray Beck opposite the White Lion at Cray. Stay to the right of the pub before turning left onto a track signed to Yockenthwaite and Stubbing Bridge.

Pass through a waymarked gate, walk through a farmyard to a second which has a sign to Yockenthwaite, and fork left onto a less distinct path leading to another sign, this time to Stubbing Bridge.

Keep to the front of a small stone house to a stile and, beyond veer diagonally leftwards down the slope towards Cray Beck, staying on the right-hand side of the stream to gain the minor road by Stubbing Bridge.

Turn right along the road for the quarter of a mile into the village of Hubberholme. By the church of St.Oswald turn left over the bridge spanning the Wharfe before swinging left again onto the lane alongside the George.

Initially river and lane keep close company and even in winter there are frequent sightings of dipper to be enjoyed. The small brown bird with its Persil-white chest often stands, flexing its legs, on boulders midstream.

By Grange Farm, which is on the right, the Wharfe swings away towards the left. Some 200 yards beyond a stone barn, turn left through a five-barred gate with a sign to Buckden Bridge. Stay to the right of a wall on a track which for a short distance has a stone surface.

On gaining the river turn right. The path loses its surface developing into a well-trodden swathe of green running along the right bank of the Wharfe until it emerges onto a minor road by Buckden Bridge. Turn left for the final 150 yards to the car park.

19. STARBOTTOM

Following a steep climb out of Kettlewell along an ancient drove road, this walk traverses high moorlands with magnificent views in all directions. The final stretch follows the Dales Way.

Route: Kettlewell – Cam Head – Starbottom – Kettlewell.

Distance: 6 miles.

Start: The Bridge car park, Kettlewell. Map reference 968722.

Map: Ordnance Survey Outdoor Leisure Map number 30, "Yorkshire Dales, Northern and Central Areas".

Public transport: Bus service number 72, Skipton-Buckden. Daily except winter Sundays. Keighley and District Bus Company.

Dalesbus service number 800, Harrogate/Leeds – Grassington – Hawes – Keld. Summer Saturdays and Sundays only. Keighley and District Bus Company and Harrogate and District Bus Company.

Dalesbus service number 809, Keighley – Hawes – Richmond. Tuesdays and Fridays only in late July and August. Keighley and District Bus Company.

Car: From Skipton take the B6265 road to Threshfield and the B6160 road from Threshfield to Kettlewell. The B6160 road leaves Wensleydale near Aysgarth to approach Kettlewell from the north. An unclassified road from Middleham approaches Kettlewell through Coverdale.

There is a large car park by the bridge at the southern entrance to Kettlewell village.

FOX AND HOUNDS, STARBOTTOM

Even the landlady, Pam Casey, is uncertain about the age of the Fox and Hounds in Starbottom but the stone lintel over the front door carries the date l834.

It provides a small cosy bar with a flagged floor, an open fire in winter, a selection of games ranging from Scrabble to Backgammon, and a special room for non-smokers. The seating is on high-backed, cushioned settles.

In the autumn of 1985 it was given the Pub of the Season award by the Keighley and Craven branch of CAMRA.

It is not surprising then that Theakston's Old Peculier, XB and Bitter are all drawn by hand pump, as is William Younger's Bitter.

Bar meals are available between midday and two o'clock.

Opening times: Tuesday, Wednesday and Thursday, 12.00 to 14.30 and 19.30 to 23.00; Friday, 19.30 to 23.00; Saturday, 12.00 to 15.00 and 19.30 to 23.00; Sunday, 12.00 to 15.00 and 19.45 to 22.30. It is closed all day Monday and at lunch time on Friday.

Kettlewell has several pubs, including The Racehorses, the Bluebell and King's Head.

The Fox and Hounds

KETTLEWELL

During the Middle Ages three great monasteries, Fountains, Bolton and Coverham, all had estates in or near Kettlewell. The result was that the village developed into an important centre in Upper Wharfedale.

From the thirteenth century it enjoyed the privilege of a weekly market. Its prosperity was further enhanced in the eighteenth and nineteenth centuries by the extensive lead mining that was developed on the surrounding fells.

Many of the fine, substantial houses still to be seen in the village were built during those two centuries. In more recent times Kettlewell has been rescued from decline by the growth of the tourist industry which is based principally on its scenic attractions.

For the walker it offers a wide range of routes from the riverside stroll to the more serious fell walk.

THE WALK

Leave the riverside car park in the direction of Kettlewell village but, opposite the Bluebell and by the Racehorses, turn right into the road signed to Leyburn. At the cross-roads by the Post Office cross directly, the narrower road now being signed to Coverdale.

Initially the gradient is steep: one in four. Follow the road round the first bend but, one hundred yards further on, where it goes through ninety degrees to the right, continue straight ahead up the wide, stoney bridleway known as Top Mere Road. It has a sign pointing to Cam Head.

With every step up the steep incline the views back down Wharfedale towards Grassington open-up further. Through a five-barred gate with a wooden seat alongside dedicated to the memory of Eric T. Sagar, the gradient eases considerably and the enormous whaleback of Great Whernside appears away to the right.

The bridleway continues as a walled lane across Cam Pastures but, after a second gate, loses the wall on the right. Soon afterwards the wall on the left turns away as well, leaving Top Mere Road to head

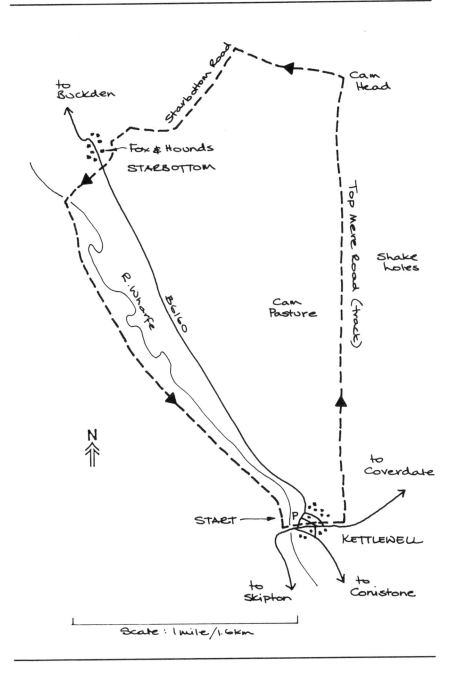

over the open moorland as a wide green trail until it meets another wall on the right.

One and a half miles out from Kettlewell it reaches Cam Head where it forms a T-junction with another bridleway, Starbottom Road. This is an ancient route heading towards Hunters Sleets before descending into Coverdale. It is worthwhile pausing at Cam Head for a few minutes to admire the view. In all directions there is a panoramic perspective as ridge after ridge of dun-coloured moorlands roll away into the far distance. It feels almost like being on top of the world.

By the finger post turn left along Starbottom Road as it swings briefly round to the north to offer tantalising glimpses of Upper Wharfedale, Langstrothdale Chase, Birks Fell, Firth Fell and Moor End Fell.

Over a ladder stile fork left with the main track, ignoring a faint path running off to the right. Through the next five-barred gate Starbottom Road becomes a walled lane and loses height rapidly while twisting down the fellside towards Starbottom village.

The last stretch, alongside Cam Gill Beck, has been concreted recently by Yorkshire Water to facilitate access to a new water treatment plant. At the first junction in the village maintain direction into a narrow street flanked by sturdy stone cottages to reach the B6160. Turn right for the final few yards to the Fox and Hounds.

Once refreshed retrace your steps along the main road, continuing almost to the edge of the village which is mentioned in Domesday Book and which was almost completely destroyed in 1686 when the worst flood in Wharfedale's history was recorded.

A few yards before the derestriction signs turn right through a five-barred gate into another walled lane signed to Kettlewell, Arncliff and Buckden. This leads directly to a sturdy footbridge over the River Wharfe. At the far end turn left through a stile to enter a meadow with the river on the left. Aim for a stile by a gateway and then stay forward to another through stile.

Ten yards beyond this climb a stile on the right but maintain direction to the right of the fence. After passing through another wall gap veer right to another stile with a gate alongside. In the next field swing further to the right, crossing a small footbridge over a stream before turning towards the left to resume walking along the river bank.

Within a short distance negotiate another stile on the right but then turn left to stay alongside the river. Over the next stile veer right again to a five-barred gate before swinging left to another small footbridge.

Over this aim for a stile some 20 yards to the right of a white gate and then keep forward to pick-up a wall on the right. Two ladder stiles in quick succession, followed by two wall gaps separated by only a few yards, lead to a five-barred gate from where the path becomes a broad green path and, eventually a walled lane. After negotiating a shallow ford turn sharp left through a wooden kissing gate onto a path which has a wall on the right and the Wharfe on the left. It is along this stretch of the river that sightings of the dipper are more than likely to be observed.

By a sign turn right through a gate and then left to walk alongside a row of trees for 150 yards before turning left through another gate. Continue to the right of the river until the path passes a finger post to meet the B6160. Turn left for the final few yards to the starting point, taking great care when crossing the road bridge.

The River Wharfe, near Starbottom

20. LINTON FALLS

A short, gentle walk through pastures and returning along a section of the Dales Way as it runs alongside the River Wharfe to one of the best-known attractions in the Dales.

Route: Grassington – High Lane – Hebden – Suspension Bridge- Linton Falls – Grassington.

Distance: 5 miles.

Start: Market Square, Grassington. Map reference 004640.

Map: Ordnance Survey Outdoor Leisure Map number 10, "Yorkshire Dales Southern Area."

Public transport: Bus service number 72, Skipton – Grassington – Buckden. Daily except for winter Sundays. Keighley and District Bus Company.

Bus service number 76, Skipton – Bolton Abbey – Grassington. Daily except Sundays. Keighley and District Bus Company.

Dalesbus service number 809, Keighley-Hawes. Summer Tuesdays and Fridays. Keighley and District Bus company.

Dalesbus service number 800, Harrogate – Leeds – Keld. Summer Tuesdays, Saturdays and Sundays. Keighley and District Bus Company.

Car: Grassington is on the B6265 road from Skipton to Hebden. It is also signed from the B6160 road at Threshfield. The Yorkshire Dales National Park has provided a large car park adjacent to the National Park Offices in Hebden Road.

THE BLACK HORSE HOTEL, GRASSINGTON

The Black Horse Hotel is an imposing black and white stone building just off Grassington's famous cobbled square.Ray and Wynn Davey offer a range of bar snacks that attract many visitors and regulars even on the most dismal of winter days. It is one of the busiest pubs in the village.

The large bar is L-shaped with plenty of wooden beams indicating its age. Built in the eighteenth century it was originally a coaching inn.Today it offers en-suite overnight accommodation. The bar is carpeted and, like many pubs in the Dales, has cushioned wall settles and a roaring log fire in winter. In summer there are tables and benches on the patio at the front of the hotel where the drinker may sit and relax, watching the world go by.

The walls are papered in white, except for the exposed stone corners of the walls. These are liberally decorated with a variety of pictures and plates, as well as old-fashioned advertisements for Fry's chocolates and Andrew's Liver Salts.

All beers are hand-drawn by pump. They include Tetley's Bitter, Theakston's Bitter, XB and Old Peculier along with Ruddle's Best Bitter.

Opening times:

Winter: weekdays, 11.00 to 15.00 and 18.00 to 23.00; Sundays, 12.00 to 15.00 and 19.00 to 22.30.
Summer: 11.00 to 23.00.

GRASSINGTON

With its country shops, cobbled Market Square, narrow streets and stone-built houses, Grassington has long been a tourist attraction. An hour spent exploring the village on foot will repay handsome dividends

Walkers are drawn to this fascinating village by the variety of routes radiating out from the centre. These range from all-day strenuous walks to short riverside ambles on easy, well waymarked paths.

Despite its size, Grassington is the real centre of Wharfedale. It lies on some of the ancient monastic routes and benefitted from the development of turnpike roads in the eighteenth century.

By that time it had also evolved as an important lead-mining centre, ore deposits being worked extensively on Grassington Moor which belonged to the Dukes of Devonshire.

Its historical importance is perhaps best illustrated by the fact that it was granted the privilege of holding a weekly market in 1282. Sadly, this declined during the nineteenth century, finally coming to an end.

Strangely, Grassington has no parish church. Along with the villages of Threshfield and Hebden, it has always been served by St. Michael's which stands about half a mile away in the beautiful village of Linton, close to the falls. This late 12th century building was remodelled and extended during the fifteenth century but is well worth a visit.

Linton Church

THE WALK

From the cobbled square in Grassington take the narrow road which climbs by the side of the Black Horse Hotel. By Lane Head cottage turn left into Scar Street but, after 100 yards and by the Congregational Church, turn right into Low Lane.

Within 50 yards, by Carrs End cottage, turn left into High Lane which has a footpath sign pointing to Hebden. This walled track climbs moderately for a short distance before levelling-off as it reaches a five-barred gate.

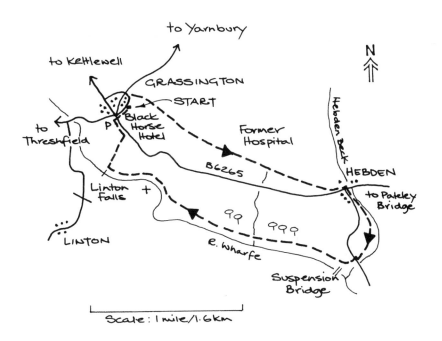

That marks the termination of the lane. It continues as a path along the edge of the next field, keeping just to the left of a wall with views across the Wharfe on your right and of Barden Fell and Simon's Seat directly ahead in the far distance.

On coming face-to-face with a large gate proclaiming "NO ACCESS" turn left, as directed, to skirt a barn on the right and then to turn right over a stile. One hundred yards further on veer left to a waymarked stile. Once over that, cross a wide track, maintaining direction across the next field to a stone step stile in the far right-hand corner and then stay about ten yards to the left of a wall until reaching another step stile. Beyond that follow the clearly defined path through a small copse of trees to reach a metalled lane by a complex of redbrick buildings. This is a former isolation hospital.

Cross the track onto a narrow tarmac path which runs across the grass of the hospital grounds and which is signed to Hebden. After 150 yards this reaches a junction in the path network. Veer slightly to the left, as waymarked, until reaching a footpath finger post, set in a narrow belt of trees, which points back towards Grassington.

Swing right by this post onto a well-defined path which works its way through the trees to a through stile. Continue straight ahead across a meadow, aiming for a gated stile and crossing directly across the track leading to Garnshaw House.

Through the stile stay about ten yards to the left of a wall until the next step stile after which the wall is replaced by a wire fence and, subsequently, another wall before continuing between two walls to a five-barred gate with a stile adjacent. From there it reverts to a walled lane leading to the road on the outskirts of Hebden village. Turn left along this to pass the Clarendon Hotel before turning right at the cross roads in the direction of Burnsall.

At the end of the school boundary wall turn left through a kissing gate which marks the start of the path signed to Hebden Suspension Bridge and Hartlington Raikes. Initially the path is cobbled. At the foot of the slope do not cross the footbridge spanning Hebden Beck but take the path to the right of the beck.

Through the first gated stile veer right over a tiny ridge to a second kissing gate and then stay forward to another footbridge over Hebden Beck close to a weir. Turn left over this and, at the far end, turn right by a wall.

By a footpath sign, cross a broad track into a green lane running to the left of some filter beds. Pass beneath some overhead power lines and, beyond two small gates, the lane becomes fenced on both sides until it emerges onto Mill Lane by Mill Bridge. Turn right over the bridge but, after 100 yards pass through a small gate on the left. Immediately fork right along the field path signed to Grassington, joining the Dales Way a short distance upstream of Hebden Suspension Bridge.

On gaining the bank of the River Wharfe turn right along the Dales Way which, at this point, passes through some of the most charming scenery in the National Park. After the third kissing gate head slightly away from the river to cross the small footbridge over Howgill Beck to another kissing gate accompanied by footpath signs. Stay ahead down a rough lane which quickly acquires a metalled surface.

A short distance beyond two cottages it bends sharply to the left. There, by a sign, go left through a stile onto a field path leading directly to Linton Falls with some fine views of St.Michael's church on the opposite bank of the Wharfe.

By Linton Falls turn right into Sedber Lane which is flagged and enclosed between walls. It leads directly to the National Park's car park and Information Centre which well repays a visit.

Leave the car park by the exit alongside the Information Centre. Turn left into Hebden Road and, at the next junction turn right into the Square to reach the Black Horse Hotel.

Linton Falls

21. HEBDEN BECK

A pleasant morning or afternoon walk over high ground to more lead mining remains before returning along the beckside path and through attractive woodlands.

Route: Hebden – High Garnshaw – New House – Hebden Beck – Hole Bottom – Hebden.

Distance: $3^3/_4$ miles.

Start: Clarendon Hotel, Hebden. Map reference 025632.

Map: Ordnance Survey Outdoor Leisure Map number 10, "Yorkshire Dales Southern Area".

Public transport: Bus service number 72, Skipton-Buckden. Daily except Sundays. Keighley and District Bus Company.

Car: Hebden is located on the B6265 road between Grassington and Pateley Bridge. There is no car park but it is possible to leave the car on the roadside. Parking at the Clarendon is for patrons only.

THE CLARENDON HOTEL

The stone-built Clarendon is to be found in the tiny village of Hebden and is sited alongside the road between Grassington and Pateley Bridge. Licensees Ken and Christine Lakin offer a warm welcome to walkers but do request that all muddy boots be removed outside the front door.

There is a cosy atmosphere in the medium-sized oblong bar with a small extra section partially partitioned-off to form a snug.Seating is on cushioned settles fixed to the white papered walls and a scattering of bar stools around wooden-topped tables.

There is plenty of brass and copperware on display as well as pictures of the Yorkshire cricket team when they last won the Sunday League. More controversial, perhaps, are the two pictures by Trog showing "The Best English" and "The Best Australian" cricket teams. No doubt they generate some fierce conversation in the bar.

Beers on offer, all drawn by hand pump, are Timothy Taylor's Best Bitter and Tetley's Bitter.

Opening times:

Summer: 11.00 to 23.00.
Winter: 11.30 to 14.30 and 19.00 to 23.00 (may be altered if business is slack.)

The Clarendon, Hebden

HEBDEN

Apart from its lead mining history the small village of Hebden has one major claim to fame.That is the impressive stone bridge spanning the beck. That was constructed to carry the turnpike road between Grassington and Pately Bridge.

THE WALK

From the Clarendon Hotel head along the B6265 in the direction of Grassington. After about 120 yards turn right into the first of two adjacent lanes which is signed to Garnshaw, Edge Lane, Tinkers' Lane and Moor Lane. It starts life with walls on either side, quickly passing to the left of a farm. At the first junction go left to pass through two five-barred gates some 20 yards apart.

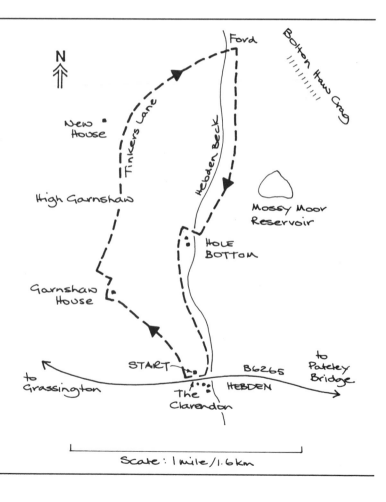

Beyond the second, turn right and, keeping to the left of a wall, climb round the corner of the field to a ladder stile in the far right-hand corner. From there maintain direction, still alongside the wall, for a further 100 yards. Then turn right through a stile in the wall. Navigational care is required at this point. Do not cross the field directly to an obvious stile in the facing wall. Instead, aim diagonally left for a more obscure ladder stile a little to the left of a gateway in the wall further up the hill.

Having negotiated this, turn right to a small gate stile which is easy to detect because there is a nearby footpath sign. Beyond this stile turn left and stay to the left of a cottage but to the right of a wall to another ladder stile. On the far side of this turn right along Tinkers' Lane, a broad grass track with a wall on the right and some breathtaking views of Wharfedale and the enclosing moorlands.

Where the wall ends in a corner continue beneath overhead power lines to a footpath junction some 100 yards ahead. Fork right, moving ever closer to the wall as you continue along the lane to pass to the left of Garnshaw House Farm and through a muddy hollow beyond.

Climb gradually to a five-barred gate with New House a short distance away to the left and with the overhead wires still running parallel on the right. Eventually the track develops into a walled lane which, after another five-barred gate, loses height, fords a small stream and corkscrews downhill to another five-barred gate in the valley bottom.

All around are more remnants of the lead mining industry which made this area so prosperous during the eighteenth and nineteenth centuries. It is amazing how so many of the spoil heaps now blend in with the surrounding landscape. Up on the moors, look out for a tall chimney, the flue from one of the abandoned smelt mills.

Ford Hebden Beck, which is shallow here except after prolonged or heavy rain. On the far bank, turn right to head downstream along a broad ex-miners' track which stays to the left of the beck. Beyond a gate there is more evidence of mining in the form of spoil heaps and flues. Despite this, the stream flows through a very attractive valley which has resumed an air of wilderness again. After three more gates, the track swings to the right over a small stone bridge and in the tiny hamlet of Hole Bottom acquires a metalled surface. Continue along it for another half mile to reach the B6265 in Hebden, Turn right for the final few yards to the Clarendon.

22. BURNSALL

This is a walk of sharp contrasts making use of several green lanes for which the Yorkshire Dales are famous. The first section traverses high, open moorland for extensive panoramic views of lower Wharfedale while the return is through lush, riverside pastures.

Route: Burnsall – Kail Lane – New Road – Parcevall Hall – Higher Skyreholme – Howgill – Burnsall.

Distance: $7^1/_2$ miles.

Start: Car park, Burnsall. Map reference 032611

Map: Ordnance Survey Outdoor Leisure Map number 10, "The Yorkshire Dales, Southern Area".

Public transport: Service number 76, Skipton – Bolton Abbey – Grassington. Daily except Sundays. Keighley and District Bus Company.

Dalesbus, service number 800. Leeds/Harrogate – Hawes. Tuesdays, Saturdays and Sundays in late July and August. Keighley and District Bus Company.

Car: Burnsall is on the B6160 road from Bolton Abbey to Threshfield. It is signed off the A59 at Bolton Abbey. There is a car park (pay on leaving) by the village green in Burnsall.

THE RED LION, BURNSALL

Long recognised as a mecca for walkers and anglers, the Red Lion occupies a delightful position adjacent to Burnsall Bridge. In summer, after a day on the surrounding hills, it is pleasant to relax at the white tables set up on the front cobbles and to look out over the village green with its tall maypole.

The large rectangular main bar is subdivided into smaller areas. It has built-in cushioned wall seats supplemented by wooden tables and Windsor chairs.

The cream coloured and panelled walls are decorated with pictures of the Barden Fell races. There is a 21b 15oz brown trout caught locally

The Maypole. Burnsall Green

on display in a glass case, a propeller from an early aeroplane, a stag's head and numerous posters advertising nineteenth century property auctions.

A smaller snug bar is served from the main one through a glass partition. Tetley's Bitter and Theakston's Bitter, both on hand pump, are served. Bar food is available lunch-time and evening.

Opening times: Monday to Saturday, 11.00 to 15.00 and 18.00 to 23.00; Sunday, 12.00 to 15.00 and 19.00 to 22.30.

The Red Lion

BURNSALL

Undoubtedly the chief glory of Burnsall is its village green, complete with maypole, set against the River Wharfe and with its elegantly proportioned arched bridge in the background. Behind range the Barden Fells.

From the Green the main street, flanked by seventeenth and eighteenth century mellowed stone houses with mullioned windows, climbs up to the church which is dedicated to St.Wilfrid of Ripon.

This dates in part from the twelfth century but for the most part is constructed in the perpendicular style of the sixteenth. Its history may be even older because it has some Viking Hog-back tombstones and there are Norse crosses carved in the style of the ninth and tenth centuries.

Inside there is a memorial tablet to Sir William Craven, a native of nearby Appletreewick, who made his fortune as a mercer and draper in London becoming, like Dick Whittington, Lord Mayor. He funded extensive repairs to Burnsall church, paid for the rebuilding of the bridge and founded the grammar school which still stands and is now used as a primary school.

One unusual feature of St. Wilfrid's is the lych-gate which has a turnstile entrance. The Burnsall Sports are held on the green annually in mid-August as they have been continuously since the reign of Elizabeth I.

Trollers Gill near Skyreholme is a deeply carved gorge, formed in the same fashion as Gordale Scar. Legend has it that it is haunted by Barguest, a ghostly dog and it was once the home of those Norse characters, the Trolls.

PARCEVALL HALL

Parcevall Hall, now a retreat and conference centre for the Diocese of Bradford, is another fine Elizabethan building. It is believed to have been used by the notorious highwayman William Nevisson who, to avoid blame for a crime near London, rode to York in under 15 hours. On arrival he played a game of bowls with the Lord Mayor, making sure that he enquired the time as he did so.In this fashion he established an alibi. His feat appeared so fantastic that King Charles II nicknamed him "Swift Nicks".

Parcevall Hall is closed to the general public but the beautiful terraced gardens are open daily from ten o'clock until six from Easter to the end of October. There is an admission charge.

THE WALK

From the car park walk across the village green towards the Red Lion. At the road junction turn right in the directions of Appletreewick. Cross the bridge and, after 50 yards, turn through a stile on the right which has a footpath finger post alongside. Strike off to the left across the grass, aiming for a small bank by the river and, having passed through a gate, stay alongside the Wharfe to reach a wooden kissing gate followed by a gated stile.

From there veer left to cross a footbridge and continue forward to reach the lane by Woodhouse Farm. Turn left along this, soon emerging onto the Burnsall to Appletreewick road.

Cross directly into Kail Lane, a sunken bridleway flanked by embankments topped with hawthorn bushes and signed to New Road. It climbs steeply onto the shoulder of Kail Hill, offering an outstanding view of Hartlington Hall to the left as it does so.

As the gradient eases it develops into a walled lane with the jagged, craggy summit of Simon's Seat clearly visible in the far distance ahead. There is another attractive view down into the clough through which the River Dibb flows on its way from Grimwith Reservoir.

By a stone barn, Kail Gate Laithe, the lane bends sharply to the left to begin a traverse of Appletreewick pastures. For a short distance the wall on the right is lost but it reappears after passing through a five-barred gate.

On reaching a cross-roads in the path network, maintain direction along the lane for a further 100 yards to another gate. Through that, advance for a few yards to a finger post and turn left along a signed bridleway with a good, firm chatter surface.

The bridleway soon reaches a ladder stile alongside a gate and then, surprisingly, passes to the left of a large, partially buried fuel tank before crossing a large stretch of rough moorland dotted with abandoned mine workings until it reaches New Road.

Turn right along this for 350 yards before climbing a ladder stile an the left to strike out along a path signed to Skyreholme. Head towards the right on the distinct path, descending gradually with a fabulous view down into Trollers Gill on the left. Beyond a ladder stile the line of the path is marked out by two parallel rows of spasmodic hawthorns.

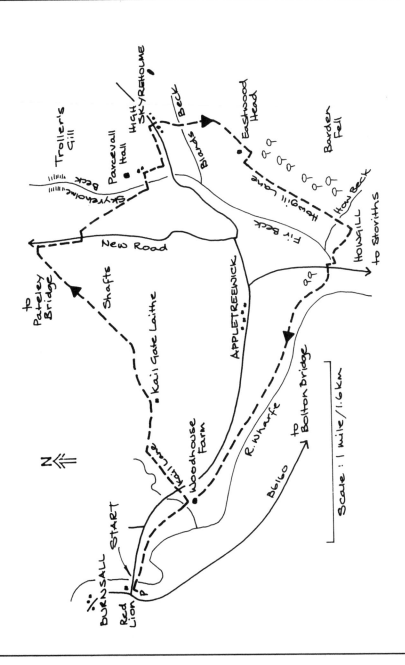

Pass above a field barn to reach a wall running along the contour. Turn right, negotiate another stile set into the facing wall in the field corner and turn left again and lose height until meeting the broad path accompanying Skyreholme Beck as it flows from Trollers Gill.

Turn right along this, pass through a five-barred gate and keep forward to the driveway to Parcevall Hall. Turn left over the bridge. After 50 yards, and in front of two cottages, turn right over a somewhat obscure step stile set into the corner to follow a field path to the left of a wall.

Beyond a gateway aim for a second and then immediately turn right through a third. Descend the field to the stile offering access to the minor road known as Skyreholme Bank. Turn left along the road for the gentle climb to Higher Skyreholme, a distance of 400 yards, at the same time keeping an eye open for a footpath finger post on the left. There, turn right through the gate opposite. Proceed between the buildings to a second gate before crossing a field, the direction indicated by the arm of another foot-path post.

Having crossed Blands Beck by means of a footbridge in the field corner, head for another step stile set into the wall on the right about half way along the field. It is located exactly where some pig wire atop the wall comes to an end.

Maintain direction through another gateway and to the left of a derelict barn to emerge onto Howgill Lane. Turn right, soon passing Eastwood Head farm with Simon's Seat now directly above to the left.

Stay with Howgill Lane for a mile. 100 yards beyond Howgill Lodge Barn and camp-site, at a cross roads in the bridleway system, turn right into another lane which descends alongside How Beck to reach the road at Howgill after a quarter of a mile.

Go right over the bridge. At the far end turn left through a stile onto the beckside path signed to Appletreewick and Burnsall. Beyond the first stile this leaves the beck to head across a field before entering Haugh Woods through a wooden kissing gate by the bank of the River Wharfe.

Stay with the well signed and waymarked path as it negotiates a succession of gates and stiles before arriving at Woodhouse Farm. From there follow the outward route back to the car park in Burnsall.

23. BOLTON ABBEY

A fascinating riverside walk with very little in the way of climbing which offers a visit to one of the most famous of all monastic sites in England combined with some delightful woodlands.

Route: Bolton Bridge – Bolton Priory – Cavendish Pavilion – The Strid – aqueduct – Posforth Bridge – Prior's Pool – Bolton Bridge.

Distance: $7^1/_2$ miles

Start: Devonshire Arms, Bolton Bridge. Map reference, 070532.

Map: Ordnance Survey Outdoor Leisure Map number 10, "Yorkshire Dales, Southern Area".

Public transport: Bus service number 76, Skipton – Bolton Abbey – Grassington.Daily except Sundays. Keighley and District Bus Company.

Dalesbus service number 800, Leeds – Grassington, Tuesdays only in late July and August. Keighley and District Bus Company.

Dalesbus service number 800, Leeds – Keld/Ingleton, Summer Saturdays only. Keighley and District Bus Company.

Dalesbus service number 800, Leeds/Harrogate – Keld, Summer Sundays and Bank Holiday Mondays. Keighley and District Bus Company. Bus service number 749, Preston – Grassington – Ilkley. Summer Sundays only. Keighley and District Bus Company.

Bus service from Skipton – Bolton Abbey – Embsay Steam Railway. Summer Sundays only. Craven Coaches.

Bus service from Ambleside to Settle – Skipton – Harrogate – York. Mondays, Wednesdays, Fridays and Saturdays only during the summer. Service is extended to Grasmere and Keswick on Saturdays only. Mountain Goat Bus Company.

Car: Bolton Bridge is on the A59 Preston to Harrogate road, It can also be reached via the B6160 road from Addingham to the south and Grassington to the north. Car parking for patrons only at the Devonshire Arms. Otherwise there is a large car park at Bolton Abbey, about a mile northwards off the B6160.

THE DEVONSHIRE ARMS

The Devonshire Arms is an upmarket Country House Hotel run by the Devonshire Estates. It looks the kind of establishment to deter many walkers from entering with their muddy boots. However, the hotel does publicise the fact that it is in prime walking country.

For the general public there is the Dukes Bar, a much more homely place with its open-cast iron stove blazing away in winter.It is L-shaped, subdivided by wooden partitions. The floor is partially carpeted and partially tiled. The bare stone walls are colour washed in cream and liberally decorated with the sporting memorabilia of Percy Braithwaite. This local worthy from Borthwick Hall was an Oxford rowing Blue, a cricketer of no mean distinction, an ace pilot during the First World War and an archaeologist to boot.

The wall settles are cushioned and supplemented with bar stools around wooden-topped tables on cast-iron legs. Beers served include Franklin's Bitter,.William Younger's Scottish Bitter and Tetley's Bitter.

Opening times: Daily, 11.00 to 23.00; Sunday, 12.00 to 23.00.

BOLTON ABBEY

Confusion surrounds the name by which these historical remains are now known. Through common usage Bolton Abbey has been applied to the ruins and the nearby village. However, strictly speaking the religious foundation was a priory, transferred to this idyllic spot from nearby Embsay in 1154.

The Augustinian Canons prospered through lead mining and sheep farming, leaving ample time for prayer, education, contempiation and serving the needs of the local community.

The priory was ransacked twice, the first time in 1318 and the second two years later, by the Scottish Border Reiver, Black Douglas. Otherwise life at Bolton Priory was normally tranquil until the Dissolution of the Monasteries in January, 1540. Thereafter much of the stone was used for local buildings but the nave remained intact to serve as a parish church. The great arch with its beautiful setting inspired several painters including Turner.

In course of time the estate passed into the possession of the Dukes of Devonshire who maintain it to this day.

Bolton Abbey

The surrounding woodlands along both banks of the Wharfe were planted by the Reverend William Carr, Vicar of Bolton Priory Church between 1789 and 1843. A man well in advance of his time, he encouraged a policy of open access to the general public. This policy is maintained by the Devonshire Estates, a small charge being made simply to meet the ever-increasing cost of maintaining the woodland paths.

The Duke of Devonshire has signed an access agreement with the Yorkshire Dales National Park for the surrounding moorlands.

THE STRID

Another famous beauty spot nearby is the Strid, a few miles upstream. It is a narrow channel through which the River Wharfe flows fast and deep. The name means literally, "the Stride", but visitors are strongly advised against attempting to leap from one bank to the other. Several people have been drowned.

THE WALK

Using the pavement, walk from the Devonshire Arms along the A59 in the direction of Harrogate. Just before Bolton Bridge turn left over a stile onto a path signed to Bolton Abbey. This begins by crossing "The Strand", an enormous waterside meadow stretching all the way to the priory ruins, a distance of $3/4$ of a mile.

The path is somewhat indistinct so aim for the gap between a small hillock on the left and the River Wharfe on the right. On passing through this gap the path becomes more distinct as it heads towards a small footbridge and then towards the left-hand corner of the Priory Church.

Cross an intersecting path, advance a few yards to a small gate and make a right turn onto a metalled driveway. This continues by the west front of the Church of St.Mary and St.Cuthbert to a second gate. Through that turn right along the path signed to Barden Bridge. Initially this stays alongside the road before passing to the right of the Cavendish Memorial Fountain, erected in memory of Lord Frederick Cavenish, one of the victims of the Phoenix Park Murders of 1882 in Dublin.

A little beyond the Memorial make a right turn down a flight of steps and then veer leftwards diagonally down the slope where the path turns northwards to run on the west bank of the Wharfe.

It soon develops into a broad track leading to the Cavendish Pavilion (refreshments) with views of Barden Fell directly ahead. Continue to the right of the Pavilion to enter Strid Woods with their multiplicity of nature trails.

Follow the green waymark along the broad ride through the beech, but, at the next junction fork right and, at the next, head left to pass a hollowed-out stone chair.

By the Information Point visit the viewing point to look at the Strid, otherwise stay forward now following a yellow waymark as the path climbs slightly and narrows to reach another junction. Ignore the steps on the right. Continue ahead still guided by the yellow waymark, to rejoin the river bank. Leave Strid Woods by a footbridge followed by a stile and head towards a castellated stone bridge which, although it is not obvious, is an aqueduct.

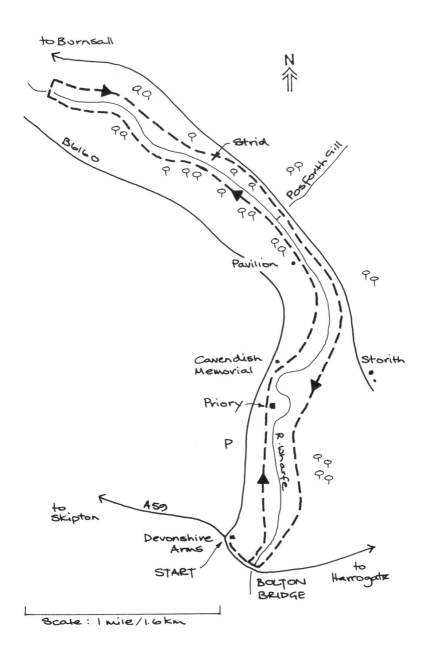

to Burnsall

N

B6160

Strid

Posforth Gill

Pavilion

Cavendish
Memorial

Storith

Priory

P

R. Wharfe

to
Skipton

A59

Devonshire
Arms

START

BOLTON
BRIDGE

to
Harrogate

Scale: 1 mile/1.6km

Cross the bridge before turning right downstream. After 100 yards head leftwards along the clear path to reach a stile before re-entering Strid Woods but now on the opposite side of the Wharfe.

At the first junction go left, especially after wet weather when the lower path is subject to flooding. Go left again at the subsequent fork to climb gently to a well constructed stone shelter .

15 yards after this, turn right to drop steeply downhill to a riverside junction. Go left along the broad track, staying with it to cross Posforth Bridge, another impressive stone affair.

At the far end turn right along a signed path to the Cavendish Pavilion. After a stile, a short flight of steps and a gate, it reaches a bridleway. To the right there is a bridge crossing the Wharfe to the Pavilion.

Unless refreshments are required ignore this. Cross directly over the bridleway onto a path signed to Bolton Priory. Continue along the riverside walking through a wide valley flanked on either side by low ridges.

After a squeezer stile turn left onto a narrow metalled road. Follow this, using the stepping stones alongside a water splash to cross a stream and then a footbridge over Pickles Gill.

Beyond, take the path on the right signed to Bolton Priory. This undulates gently through the woods but, just before dropping to Waterfall Bridge near the Priory, reaches a junction.

Fork left along another path signed to Storiths. At the top of the short rise, fork right and after 40 yards negotiate a stile. Keep to the left of a fence and cross two small footbridges before dropping through a pasture to another stile followed by another footbridge.

Stay forward over the next field but, after a five-barred gate take the broad track which climbs to pass through some trees where the river forms a large bend to the right.

Over another stile remain to the left of a fence before returning to river level. Beyond the next stile the path is flanked by a wall and a hedge for the final short distance to the A59.

Turn right along the road, cross the concrete footbridge and stay with the road to return to the Devonshire Arms.

24. KIRKBY MALHAM

A walk through gently undulating pastures Which offers wide-ranging views of upper Airedale and the surrounding hills.

Route: Kirkby Malham – Kirk Gait – Warber Hill – Dowber Laithe – Scosthrop Lane – Airton – Kirkby Malham.

Distance: 4$^{1}/_{2}$ miles

Start: Victoria Inn, Kirkby Malham. Map reference 895609

Map: Ordnance Survey Outdoor Leisure Map number 10, "Yorkshire Dales, Southern Area".

Public transport: Bus service number 210, Skipton to Malham via Gargrave. Daily except winter Sundays. Pennine Buses.

Car: Kirkby Malham is located on the minor road from Gargrave to Malham. Malham is signed off the A65 in the centre of Gargrave.

THE VICTORIA INN, KIRKBY MALHAM

As in so many villages the Victoria Inn, Kirkby Malham, is adjacent to

the church. Its bright and cheerful lounge bar has a long, fitted and upholstered wall bench plus wooden-topped tables with stools.

The cream coloured walls, appropriately, carry pictures of Queen Victoria and four Dickensian type paintings of the four seasons. There are several photographs of local scenes, a badger's head, items of horse harness and an oil lamp. There is a separate, more plainly furnished and much smaller tap room. On offer in both, all hand drawn, are Tetley's Bitter, Younger's Scotch Bitter and Theakston's Bitter. Bar meals are served at lunch-time and in the evening.

Sundial, Victoria Inn

Opening times: Monday to Saturday, 12.00 to 15.00 and 19.00 to 23.00; Sunday, 12.00 to 15.00 and 19.00 to 22.30. In winter, apart from the Christmas season, the Victoria does not open at lunch times except on Fridays, Saturdays and Sundays.

As the name implies, Kirkby Malham is the ecclesiastical centre of Malhamdale. The fine church of St. Michael and All Angels serves a parish of 35 square miles. This includes Malham, Otterburn, Scosthrop and Airton. The scattered population totals 500. A charter, dated 1199, granted the parish to the monks of West Dereham in Norfolk, a gift from Adam of Giggleswick. They continued to enjoy the benefice until the Reformation.

The church itself occupies the site of a pre-Norman religious foundation. The present building is of the fifteenth century, its fine oak roof showing the Norfolk influence of the monks of West Dereham.

The interior is wide and spacious, the nave being separated from the side aisles by rows of columns, some of which have niches once occupied by statues of saints. Two of the columns also have weird carved stone heads. There are box pews.

Outside the south west buttress of the tower carries the coats of arms of four local families while the south east buttress is decorated with those of Fountains Abbey, once a large landowner in the area.

The door in the south porch has a sanctuary ring and above this is a modern sculpture of St. Michael slaying the dragon. Opposite the south door is the Devil's Door, so-called because it was left open during baptisms so that any evil spirits could be driven out by the Holy Spirit.

In the Lady Chapel there is a modern memorial of Lakeland stone in memory of John Lambert of nearby Calton Hall who became a general in the Parliamentary Army during the Civil War.

THE WALK

Take the lane alongside the front of the Victoria. After 50 yards, and opposite the church, turn left by a footpath sign to cross Kirkby Beck by a stone footbridge before ascending a flight of steps to a wooden gate. From there head for a step stile in the wall on the right before crossing the next field leftwards to a waymarked stile in the diagonally opposite corner.

Head uphill, keeping to the left of a fence and, subsequently, of a small wood from where there are extensive views over towards Cracoe Fell.

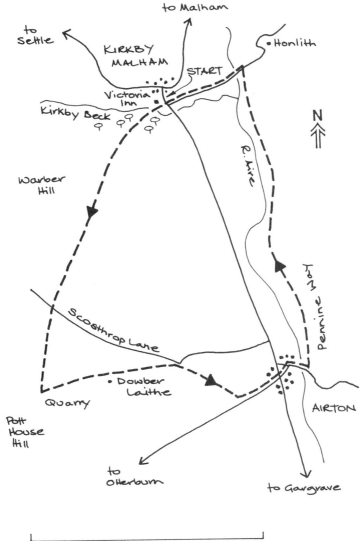

to Malham

to Settle

KIRKBY MALHAM

• Honlith

START

Victoria Inn

Kirkby Beck

R. Aire

Warber Hill

Scosthrop Lane

Pennine Way

N

Quarry

• Dowber Laithe

Pott House Hill

AIRTON

to Otterburn

to Gargrave

Scale : 1 mile / 1.6 km

By the far corner of the wood negotiate the stile in the facing fence before advancing over a large pasture known as Kirk Gait, all the time bearing left to a stone footbridge which is not immediately obvious but which is close to Deepdale plantation.

Across that climb for 20 yards to a step stile in the wall on the right. Turn left and, staying to the right of another wall, climb gently up the shoulder of Warber Hill with High Ings barn visible to the right.

At a footpath junction, recognised by a finger post, maintain direction to reach another step stile a little to the right of a small copse. Stay with the wall but, where this corners away to the left, continue forward to meet another wall passing to the right of a small abandoned quarry and a white enamel bath set into a stone water trough on the way.

From this point onwards the path becomes more distinct as it descends the slope to meet Scosthrop Lane.

Cross directly to a ladder stile to start the gentle climb of a sloping meadow, taking direction from the arm of the finger post. On gaining the crest of the hill, aim for the wall corner on the left before advancing forward to the right of a wall. To the right is an excellent view of Great Houber Hill.

Five yards after the next stile, which has concrete blocks for steps, turn left over a ladder stile. Aim to the left of a small copse of coniferous trees which marks the site of a disused quarry and then stay forward along the broad grassy path to a five-barred gate a few yards to the left of a small stone barn marked on the map as Dowber Laithe.

Advance up the hill before swinging left towards a makeshift sheep-fold in the far corner of the field. Negotiate this by a series of small gates, as indicated by an arrow, to regain Scosthrop Lane.

Turn right for 300 yards. Where the narrow lane corners left through ninety degrees, turn right through a five-barred gate onto a bridleway signed to Town End.

Pass to the right of a stone barn, negotiate a second 5-barred gate and stay to the right of a row of trees on what appears to be a raised embankment along the field boundary. After the next gate there is a wall on the left as the track continues in a direct line to emerge onto the road linking Airton with Otterburn.

Turn left along the road to enter Airton village. Cross the main Gargrave to Malham road, advancing to the right of the attractive village green before dropping down the hill to a stone bridge spanning the Aire. Keep an eye open for the house with the built-in dovecote.

At the far end of the bridge turn left into a short track. After 15 yards, and by the water's edge, go right over the stile onto the riverside path signed as the Pennine Way.

Beyond the second gated stile cross the small footbridge over Foss Gill before turning sharp right as signed. At this point the Aire is a short distance away to the left as the path traverses rough pastureland which is noted as a breeding ground for wading birds in spring and early summer.

As the path negotiates two small gates separated by a mere ten yards it is rejoined by the river. From that point stay to the left of a derelict house to a wooden kissing gate and keep alongside the Aire to reach the stone bridge which carries the Hanlith road. On the approach to this there is a good view of Hanlith Hall.

Negotiate the stile alongside the bridge before turning left along the road, known as Green Gate, for the final quarter of a mile into Kirkby Malham.

Pennine Way sign, Airton

25. MALHAM

This walk visits all the well-known geological features which have created Malham's reputation as a tourist centre.

Route: Malham – Janet's Foss – Gordale Scar – Smearbottoms Lane – Mastiles Lane – Malham Tarn – Malham Cove – Malham.

Distance: 10 miles.

Start: Buck Inn, Malham. Map reference 891627.

Map: Ordnance Survey Outdoor Leisure Map number 10, "Yorkshire Dales, Southern Area".

Public transport: Bus service number 210, Skipton – Gargrave – Malham. Daily except winter Sundays. Pennine Bus Company.

Car: Malham is reached by a minor road signed from the A65 in the centre of Gargrave. There is a large National Park car park on the southern edge of the village.

THE BUCK, MALHAM

Undoubtedly the biggest pub in Malham, the Buck stands in the village centre alongside the main road. It has long been a mecca for tourists as well as walkers.

There is a large, well-furnished and carpeted lounge bar but, more important perhaps, it has a separate, L-shaped Hikers' Bar with its bare floors and unadorned white walls. There are no carpets on the floor.

The Buck offers en-suite accommodation and bar meals.

Beers include Whitbread's Trophy Bitter, Boddington's Bitter, Theakston's Bitter, Theakston's XB and Theakston's Old Peculier, all on hand pump.

Opening times: Summer, 11.00 to 23.00; Winter, 11.00 to 15.00 and 19.00 to 23.00.

The Buck Inn

SOURCE OF THE AIRE

Malham Beck, featured at the beginning of this walk, is not the source of the River Aire. It is the stream which bubbles out from the base of Malham Cove where it provided Charles Kingsley with the germ of the idea later developed into his classic work, "The Water Babies".

The Aire originates much higher in Malham Tarn before vanishing underground at Water Sinks. It next appears on the surface at Aire Head, a short distance south of Malham village and beyond the first turn of this walk.

JANET'S FOSS

Janet's Foss is a small, pretty waterfall cascading down through the trees. Until recent times the pool at the foot of the fall was used by local farmers as a sheepwash. The veil of water hides a cave, legendary home of Janet, Queen of the local fairies.

GORDALE SCAR

The result of a collapsed cave system, Gordale Scar is cathedral-like in its proportions. Justifiably it is regarded as a classic geological formation attracting students from many parts of the world. Notice, too, the extensive beds of water-cress growing in the clear waters of the beck. At the far end of the gorge there is a view of the two-tiered waterfall, a splendid spectacle after heavy rain.

MALHAM TARN

Malham Tarn is one of only two natural lakes in the limestone areas of the Yorkshire Dales, the other being Semerwater in Wensleydale. It is formed by a natural hollow beneath which is a bed of impervious Silurian slate. At its neck the water is impounded by a moraine of glacial debris.

The tarn and surrounding land is owned by the National Trust which has developed it as a nature reserve noted for its wildfowl and other avian species.

On the far side of the tarn is Malham Tarn House. Built as a shooting lodge, it is now used as a field study centre offering courses in a variety of subjects. It was while staying there that Charles Kingsley penned his classic, "The Water Babies".

MALHAM COVE

The enormous semi-circular limestone cliff just above Malham village forms a gigantic natural amphitheatre. It is the best surface manifestation of the Craven Fault, a geological feature resulting from movements of the earth's crust in prehistoric times.

The cove is topped by an extensive limestone pavement consisting of flat blocks known as "clints" and intersected by deep fissures or "grikes". The grikes, formed by persistent water action, are renowned for their wild flora including hart's tongue fern and dog's mercury, species more usually associated with woodlands.

THE WALK

Cross the stone footbridge spanning Malham Beck almost opposite the front door of "The Buck" before turning right along the footpath signed to Janet's Foss and Gordale Scar.

After two stiles and a succession of waterside meadows that are a botanist's paradise in summer, pass through a kissing gate to reach a junction immediately. Turn left onto the path to Janet's Foss.

This skirts to the left of a stone barn before continuing with a wall on the right to another kissing gate. Beyond this a sequence of stiles leads to the entrance of Janet's Foss Woodlands. Since 1982 these have formed part of the National Trust's Malham Tarn Estate. They consist principally of ash and hazel which have regenerated naturally since the last ice age.

In Spring they are carpeted with wild garlic and dog's mercury but their chief glory is "Lords and Ladies", otherwise known by a variety of names including "Sweethearts", "Adam and Eve" or "Cuckoo Pint". They flower in April and May, subsequently developing clusters of highly poisonous red berries.

Continue along the well-constructed path through the woodlands as far as Janet's Foss. Climb with it to the left of the waterfall to Gordale Lane. Turn right along the road to Gordale Bridge. 300 yards beyond turn left through a gate onto another surfaced path leading through Gordale Scar.

Proceed to the far end of the gorge for a view of the waterfall. It is possible to scramble up the side of this before joining a continuation of the path towards Malham Tarn. However, this course is not recommended for the inexperienced or if the beck is in full spate.

Instead, retrace your steps to Gordale Lane. Turn left into the road which quickly changes its name to Hawthorn Lane. Although metalled, it carries very little traffic running, as it does, only as far as Lee Gate House.

For the first half mile Hawthorn Lane climbs very steeply before levelling out to become Smearbottoms Lane, a medieval monastic route travelled by the monks of Fountains Abbey who controlled extensive sheep ranges in the Malham area.

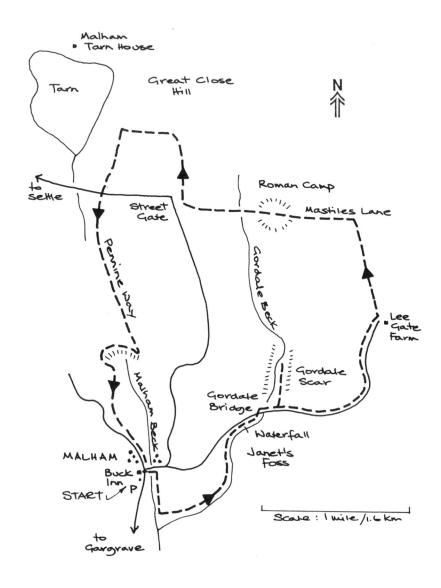

For well over a mile ignore any side paths or bridleways, inviting though these may seem. Where the tarmac ends, directly opposite Lee Gate House, make a left turn through a five-barred gate with a green footpath sign alongside.

After a somewhat muddy start, this path becomes clear and easy to follow just to the right of a wall. After $3/4$ of a mile over green upland pasture, pass through another five-barred gate onto Mastiles Lane, perhaps the best-known of all monastic routes through the Dales. Immediately turn left to negotiate another five-barred gate before proceeding along Mastiles Lane with a wall on the left and magnificent views in all directions. Sadly much of the surface has become rutted because of over-use by four-wheel-drive vehicles.

Although the site can easily be missed, Mastiles Lane passes through the very centre of a Roman Camp, now a grassy mound, before crossing Gordale Beck by an ancient clapper bridge. It then climbs gradually to Street Gate on Malham Moor where it acquires a metalled surface.

Through another five-barred gate turn right onto the signed bridleway heading towards Great Close Hill. After a quarter of a mile, and immediately before a cattle grid, turn left onto a grassy path skirting the left-hand side of Great-Close Plantation.

Stay to the left of the wall and, where this ends, remain to the left of the subsequent fence to meet the broad track leading to Malham Tarn, now clearly visible away to the right.

Cross the broad track before veering leftwards towards the corner of a wood on the right to meet the Pennine Way. Turn left along this, passing beneath some overhead wires to the narrow metalled road which is a continuation of Mastiles Lane heading towards Settle.

Cross directly onto the green track leading to a ladder stile. Just beyond this, at a signed footpath junction, head to the left of some pools before resuming direction between two small limestone outcrops, still with the Pennine Way.

Beyond a ladder stile on the boundary of National Trust land the path becomes rocky as it drops abruptly through a wall gap to a ladder stile.

This section is noteworthy for the line of molehills which appear to indicate that these underground burrowers are following the course of the path.

At the next finger post turn acutely right following the waymarked path downhill to a ladder stile. Over that take as direct a line as possible across the limestone pavement located above Malham Cove. On the far side climb either of the twin ladder stiles before descending the stepped path to the right of the cove's sheer limestone face.

Malham Cove

On reaching the cove floor fork left to walk to the foot of the cove face. Retrace your steps to the junction, this time forking left again along the surfaced path which, after two gates, reaches Cove Road. Turn left downhill to regain Malham village and the Buck Inn.

PROBLEMS

Malham has so many natural and geological features that it was attracting visitors long before the National Park was established. Today it has developed into a honeypot village which experiences overcrowding problems at busy periods.

To cope with the pressures, the National Park authority has created a large car park at the southern end of the village and built an Information Centre which has recently updated its displays. Plans are in hand for enlarging the car park.

The village itself, built of mellowed stone houses, some of them colour washed, is an attraction in itself with numerous clapper bridges spanning the beck.

The Limestone Pavement

26. STAINFORTH FORCE

A linear route linking the ancient market town of Settle with Horton-in-Ribblesdale. For much of the way it follows riverside paths and provides excellent views of Stainforth Force and Stainforth Bridge.

Route: Settle – Langcliffe – Stainforth Force – Little Stainforth – Helwith Bridge – Horton-in-Ribblesdale.

Distance: 7 miles.

Start: Golden Lion, Settle. Map reference 816637

Finish: Horton-in-Ribblesdale station. Map reference 804727

Map: Ordnance Survey Outdoor Leisure Map number 2, "Yorkshire Dales Western Area".

Public transport: Settle is on the Settle – Carlisle line. Daily services between Leeds and Carlisle except on winter Sundays. On certain summer Sundays there are also direct services from Stockport, Blackpool, Manchester and Preston.

Details of time table from British Rail: Leeds 448133; Carlisle 44711; Skipton 792543.

Horton-in-Ribblesdale is on the same line. For details, see above and also the walk from Horton-in-Ribblesdale.

Bus service number 590, Settle – Skipton – Keighley. Monday to Saturday. No Sunday service. Skipton Busways.

Bus service number 580, Skipton – Settle – Ingleton. Daily all year. Pennine Bus Company.

Bus service number 98X, Leeds – Grasmere. Summer Sundays only. Keighley and District Bus Company.

Bus services numbers 110 and 111, Clitheroe – Settle. Tuesdays only. Lakeland coaches.

Bus service from Keswick to York. Summer service on Mondays, Wednesdays, Fridays and Saturdays. Mountain Goat Bus Company.

Car: Settle is signed from the A65(T) Skipton to Kendal road. There are two large car parks near the town centre.

THE GOLDEN LION, SETTLE

Although well maintained, the exterior of the Golden Lion fronting onto Duke Street provides no clue to the interior of the bar. Stepping through the door is like stepping into a completely different world. It resembles the impressive entrance hall of a stately mansion with panelled plaster ceiling, two pillars and a wide, polished and carpeted wooden staircase rising almost out of the middle of the floor.

There is also a large recessed stone fireplace with wooden surrounds in which, if the weather is cold, there is always a log fire blazing exuding a warm welcome that is so typical of the hospitality provided by Joan and Bernard Houghton.

Walk in during the festive season and you will not be surprised to learn that it has won several awards for the pub with the best Christmas decorations in the North West. In addition to a fine restaurant it also serves bar food at lunchtime and in the evenings. Thwaites Bitter and other ales are matured in the cellar.

Opening times: Monday to Saturday, 11.00 to 15.00 and 18.00 to 23.00. Sundays, 12.00 to 15.00 and 19.00 to 22.30.

SETTLE

Settle is a fascinating small town with its imposing town hall overlooking the Market Square. The charter according it the privilege of holding a weekly market dates back to 1249 and even to this day the Square is packed with brightly coloured stalls every Tuesday. For centuries it has been the agricultural focus of the area, the meeting place between the sheep farming of the uplands and the arable farming of the lower Ribble valley.

Its prosperity was further enhanced in the late eighteenth century by the growth of several small manufacturing industries, evidence of which may still be seen amongst the buildings standing in the narrow streets and small courtyards. None of the national chain-stores have moved into the town. The shops for the most part remain independently owned, often having been in the same family for generations. This alone helps to create a warm, friendly atmosphere.

Opposite to Ye Olde Naked Man cafe (formerly an inn) on the Square is a group of shops known as The Shambles, but perhaps the most famous building is Preston's Folly dating back to 1675 .

Many of the inns and hotels were built to cater for the needs of travellers when the road from Keighley to Kendal was turnpiked in the eighteenth century. Settle enjoys a milder climate than many parts of the Yorkshire Dales because it is protected in the east by Constitution Hill and Attermire Scar, both visible surface indications of the mid-Craven Fault which extends from Settle to Malham.

Today the town is closely associated with the famous railway line which runs northwards to Carlisle through some of the most spectacular scenery in England. British Rail's plans to force closure have thankfully been thwarted through the efforts of various pressure groups. It is a useful artery not only for rail enthusiasts and ramblers, but also for the people who live in many of the small and scattered communities of the Dales.

Settle Station

THE WALK

From the Golden Lion walk along Duke Street to the Market Place and then continue forward along the Kendal road to the stone bridge spanning the River Ribble. By the far end of this, having crossed the

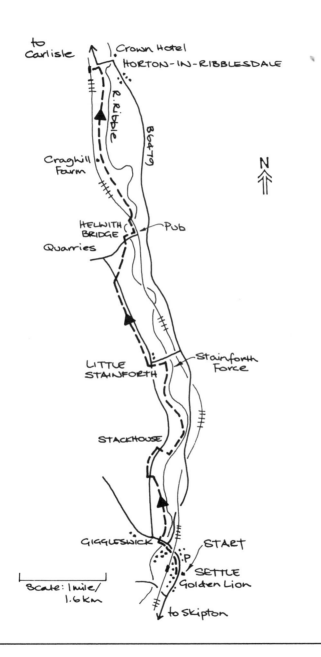

Giggleswick boundary, turn right along a well maintained footpath signed to Stackhouse. There is a football pitch to the right and a rugby field to the left. The path reaches the fenced bank of the Ribble within 200 yards but then corners to the left, acquiring a wall on the right at the same time.

30 yards after the corner negotiate a stile on the right, walk across the centre of a large field to a gated stile and then, staying to the right of a wall followed by a fence, advance to two more stiles. After the second veer slightly leftwards to a third which allows access to the minor road leading to Stackhouse.

Cross more or less directly to a stile with a Ribble Way sign alongside. Turn sharp right, separated from the road by nothing more than a stone wall. In the far corner of the field turn right over a stile to regain the road.

Turn left to enter the tiny hamlet of Stackhouse after 200 yards. By the far corner of a white house on the right, "Ribblelands", turn right into a walled lane heading in the direction of Attermire Scar. This leads to a footbridge over the Ribble within a quarter of a mile. Do not cross. Turn left to negotiate, within ten yards, a stile signed to Stainforth Bridge.

The delightful riverside path is well-used and so easy to follow as it uses a variety of stiles one of which, uniquely perhaps, has the stump of a tree as a step. By a mill, located on the far bank of the river and with the sheer face of a disused quarry as a backcloth, the path traverses a delightful grass terrace between the river and a mixed woodland of beech and oak on the left. Mallard are rarely absent and there can be occasional sightings of the restless dipper and the patient heron standing vigilant for a sighting of his unsuspecting prey.

On reaching a caravan site keep to the right of the five-barred entrance gate to a ladder stile beyond which is Stainforth Force, a delightful series of cascading waterfalls where, in late summer and autumn it is possible to catch glimpses of leaping salmon.

A few yards upstream is the graceful stone arch of Stainforth Bridge, reflected in the calm waters of the river. Now under the protection of the National Trust, this was built in 1675 by Samuel Watson of nearby Knight Stainforth Hall, to improve the packhorse route through Ribblesdale.

Having negotiated the stile by the bridge turn left along the metalled road into Little Stainforth. On the approach notice the unusual weather vane on the first building. It is a cow – a Craven Heifer no doubt!

By Knight Stainforth Hall on the right, which was built by Watson at the same time as the bridge, there is a T. junction. Turn right along what is little more than a walled lane with a surface. This climbs almost imperceptibly to pass Banks Barn and Leys Barn before finally presenting a splendid view of Pen-y-ghent away to the right and, a little more distant, of Ingleborough.

Soon after the going levels the road becomes unfenced and passes beneath two sets of overhead power lines. Almost immediately beyond the second fork right onto an unsigned bridleway by Sunnybank Barn to cross open country before reaching the road from Helwith Bridge to Austwick. Basically it is a minor road but has been widened at this point to accommodate quarry traffic.

Turn right for the quarter of a mile into the village of Helwith Bridge where it is possible to quench one's thirst at the Helwith Bridge Hotel.

Otherwise, turn left by the far corner of the school into another metalled lane which is signed to Arcow Quarry. After a quarter of a mile, where the lane turns through ninety degrees to the left, turn right through a five-barred gate to pass beneath a railway bridge into a walled lane. Ignore a footbridge over the Ribble , staying forward to the right of a wall and again, where the river bends to the right, continue straight ahead, still with the walled lane.

Over a ladder stile walk along a walled ditch for a short distance before taking aim for a wall corner on the left. This reunites the path with the river. Turn left along the river bank to pass to the right of Craghill Farm before gaining a ladder stile. From here the stiled path stays along the left bank of the Ribble until it reaches the B6479 by the bridge at Horton-in-Ribblesdale. Turn left for the short distance to Horton station and the train journey back to Settle. There is something rather enjoyable about sitting on the train and looking through the window at many parts of the route just walked.

For anyone seeking refreshments in Horton before catching the train there is the Crown Hotel (see Horton-in-Ribblesdale walk) or the Pen-y-ghent cafe which caters specially for walkers.

27. HORTON-IN-RIBBLESDALE

A linear walk across some of the bleakest yet most attractive moorlands in the Yorkshire Dales. The route also crosses an ancient packhorse bridge and allows for a return journey on the famous Settle-Carlisle railway line.

Route: Horton-in-Ribblesdale – Sell Gill – Beckwith Moor – Old Ing – Ling Gill – Cam End – Ribblehead station. Return to Horton-in-Ribblesdale by train.

Distance: $8^1/_2$ miles

Start: Crown Hotel, Horton-in-Ribblesdale. Map reference 808727.

Finish: Ribblehead Station. Map reference 766790.

Map: Ordnance Survey Outdoor Leisure Map number 2, "Yorkshire Dales, Western Area."

Train: Both Horton-in-Ribblesdale (start) and Ribblehead (finish) are served by the Settle-Carlisle railway line. There are daily services throughout the year between Leeds and Carlisle, including summer Sundays. There are no trains on winter Sundays.

Details of services from British Rail: Leeds 448l33: Carlisle 44711: Skipton 792543.

Friends of the Settle – Carlisle Railway publish seasonal time-tables, which may be obtained from all stations on the line, National Park Information Centres and Tourist Information Centres in the areas served.

Buses: Bus service number 805, Settle – Horton-in-Ribblesdale. Daily except Sundays. Whaites Coaches and Keighley and District Bus Company.

Car: Signed from the centre of Settle, Horton-in-Ribblesdale is located on the B6479, Settle to Ribblehead road. There is a Yorkshire Dales National Park car park close to the Crown Hotel.

THE CROWN HOTEL

Strangers to Horton-in-Ribblesdale may well be excused for being perplexed by the location of the Crown Hotel, a white-fronted building which stands alongside the bridge carrying the B6479 over the Ribble. The Ordnance Survey marks the spot with the words, "New Inn".

Many people conclude that there has been a name change and the map is in need of revision. Landlady Norma Hargreaves avers, however, that this is not the case. The name "New Inn" refers to the area of land immediately adjacent to the bridge on either side of the river. There has never been a hostelry of that name on the site.

The Crown itself is of ancient origin, dating back to the seventeenth century when it was both a farm and an inn serving thirsty drovers leading their cattle along the ancient trackways of the Dales to the markets of Lancashire and beyond. As a farm it would also provide grazing.

In the eighteenth and nineteenth centuries it prospered as a coaching inn on the turnpike which ran from Settle to Gearstones at Ribblehead where it joined the Richmond to Lancaster Turnpike.

Today it accommodates Pennine Wayfarers. It is also a rendezvous for both the walkers and cavers who flock into this attractive limestone area. It is ideally situated for an ascent of Pen-y-ghent, Ingleborough and even Whernside.

The Crown has two bars, one small, the other slightly larger. Both have open fires when the weather is inclement. There are wooden beams and the walls are lined with cushioned wooden settles. The spacious garden has chairs and tables for use when the weather is fine and also seating outside at the front. Bar meals are served at lunch-time and in the evenings. For those in search of something a little more formal there is a restaurant although bow ties are not mandatory.

In summer, Theakston's Bitter, XB and Old Peculier are on offer along with Younger's Scottish Bitter. In winter, when the demand is less, old Peculier is withdrawn because of its poor lasting qualities.

Opening times: Daily 11.00 to 15.00 and 18.00 to 23.00; on Saturdays, Bank Holidays and other busy days during the summer it tends to remain open from 11.00 to 23.00, depending on custom.

THE WALK

Take the bridleway to the right of the Crown Hotel signed as the Pennine Way. This was formerly a packhorse route linking Horton-in-Ribblesdale with Cam End and Hawes.

Initially the climbing is fairly steep but eases off for a while after a quarter of a mile. On days when visibility is good Ingleborough may be seen to the left and Pen-y-ghent to the right. After a ladder stile the walled lane dips slightly to cross a stream before resuming its climb to a five-barred gate.

At this point look for the Sell Gill Holes, one on either side of the track. Both are favourites with experienced cavers and are the first of several to be passed on this walk.

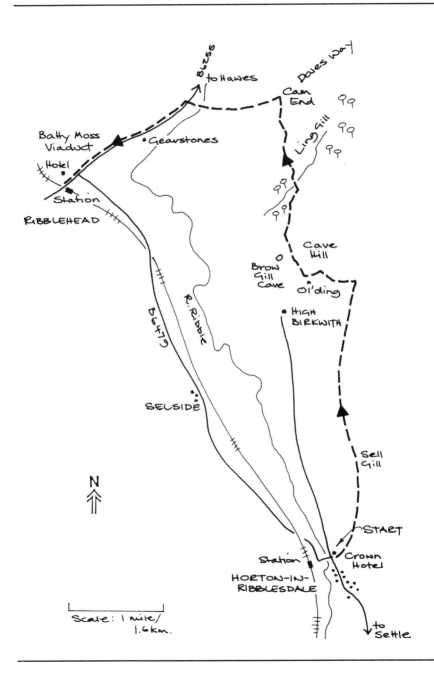

Through the gate stay with the bridleway, ignoring an indistinct path branching off to the left and signed to Birkwith. The going eases as the Pennine Way develops into a wide green lane contouring round Sell Gill Hill and Jackdaw Hill before passing Red Moss Pot.

This is a glorious extensive landscape of open moorland with a true wilderness atmosphere. Even in winter the grouse are never silent.

For much of the way there is a stone wall on the left but, after almost two miles the track swings right to ford a broad stream flowing off Birkwith Moor. After heavy or prolonged rain it can be quite deep.

The problem of crossing is solved, however, by a large limestone slab firmly embedded in the ground a few yards to the right. This more or less completely overhangs the entire width of the water.

Once across proceed through the facing five-barred gate, maintaining direction but looking out for a small concrete tablet on the left bearing the inscription, "Thornton and Garnett".

After the next five-barred gate turn left onto a narrower but obvious path indicated by the Pennine Way sign. This climbs briefly to the crown of a hill which commands a breathtaking view of Ingleborough, Whernside, upper Langstrothdale and the head of the Ribble Valley.

Stay forward over slightly boggy ground, descending gently to a ladder stile. Continue straight ahead, now with a wall on the immediate left to a T-junction.

Turn left along a broad lane with a hard surface of compacted stone chippings with Old Ing Farm just over the wall on the left. This, overlooked by Dismal Hill, has been weathered by the centuries for it is frequently featured in eighteenth century travellers' guide books.

By the farm negotiate another gate to a second T-junction. Turn right into a walled lane with a rocky surface. This is another ancient packhorse route which, at some time in the eighteenth century appears to have been improved to become part of the recommended road for travellers between London and Askrigg. Today it carries the Pennine Way. By the first five-barred gate is the famous Calf Gill pot-hole. This has a stream thundering over its edge into a subterranean passage from which it emerges at Browgill Cave a short distance away to the left.

The stoney track wends its way along the contours of Cave Hill and Fair Bottom Hill before descending alongside Ling Gill National Nature Reserve.

This is now but a fragment of a once extensive high level deciduous woodland. The prime tree species are ash, wych elm, birch, rowan, bird cherry, aspen, hawthorn and hazel, all preserved because the flanks of this limestone gorge are too precipitous for sheep to graze.

It also boasts a notable and varied ground flora of which globe flower and melancholy thistle are the prize attractions. Permits to visit the reserve are available from English Nature. Within a few yards of the northern end of the reserve the bridleway crosses Ling Gill bridge, a very attractive stone structure set in a true wilderness. It repays careful examination for it has a faint inscription saying that when it was rebuilt in 1765 it was "at the charge of the whole West Riding".

From the bridge the track, rough and rocky once again, climbs gradually back onto the open moors between Small Bank and Long Bank to a T-junction at Cam End. Turn left along an even broader track signed to Holme End. Note that this is the parting of the ways because the Pennine Way heads off in the opposite direction.

Our direction, however, is a section of the Dales Way using what was originally a Roman road, the Cam High Road, linking Ingleton with Bainbridge in Wensleydale. During the eighteenth century it was turnpiked as part of the Richmond to Lancaster route but later abandoned.

With the famous Ribblehead Viaduct directly ahead the track loses height rapidly and in a little under a mile reaches a wooden footbridge over Gayle Back. At the far end veer slightly left to an obvious ladder stile in the facing wall before keeping to the left of a wall to another stile and the B6255.

Turn left to pass Gearstones, a former drovers' inn and the setting for two annual cattle fairs. At the road junction stay forward to the Station Hotel and turn left into the approach to Ribblehead station for the train back to Horton-in-Ribblesdale.

If time allows take the path near the hotel to enjoy a closer inspection of the Ribblehead Viaduct or, to give it its correct name, the Batty Moss Viaduct. (For details see the Ingleborough walk).

Ribblehead Viaduct, with the 'Mallard' locomotive in full steam

THE STATION HOTEL, RIBBLEHEAD

One of the most isolated pubs in the Yorkshire Dales, the Station Hotel stands in one of the National Park's bleakest landscapes, a high plateau of moorland dominated by Ingleborough and Whernside.

At the end of this walk it provides an ideal opportunity for a pint and, perhaps, a bar meal while waiting for the train. Like most pubs in the Dales it has a beamed ceiling and wooden settle seating with some provision for outdoor drinking when the weather permits. It has a semi-circular bar just inside the entrance with a larger room, complete with pool table, on the right. The walls are adorned with photographs of the Settle-Carlisle railway, especially of trains at Ribblehead itself.

For the thirsty walker there is a choice between Theakston's Bitter, Younger's Scotch Bitter and Younger's Pale Ale. Not surprisingly in this wilderness area the opening hours tend to be rather fluid with all day opening during the summer months and at week-ends.

28. CRUMMACK DALE

A classic walk through limestone country with some geological rarities. It makes extensive use of traditional green lanes.

Route: Austwick – Norber Erratics – Nappa Scar – Crummack Dale – Long Scar – Long Lane – Thwaite Lane – Austwick.

Distance: $8^1/_4$ miles

Start: The Game Cock, Austwick. Map reference 768685

Map: Ordnance Survey Outdoor Leisure Map number 2, "Yorkshire Dales Western Area".

Public transport: Bus service number 580, Skipton-Settle-Ingleton. Daily including Sundays. Pennine Bus Company.

Bus Service numbers 279 and 281, Settle-Lancaster.Daily except Sundays. Lancaster City Transport.

Dalesbus service number 809, Keighley-Settle, Tuesdays and Fridays in late July and August. Keighley and District Bus Company.

Car: Austwick is signed from the A65, Skipton to Kendal road south of Ingleton and north of Settle. There is no official car park but there is a limited amount of roadside parking in the village. The Game Cock has limited parking for patrons only.

THE GAME COCK, AUSTWICK

This small unpretentious pub has one of the friendliest atmospheres to be found in the Dales. The tiny, square bar is beamed while the butter-coloured walls are decorated with prints of cock fighting.

There is one unusual poster. It is advertising that the Game Cock will open its doors at four o'clock in the morning for the benefit of anyone wishing to witness the solar eclipse on 29th July, 1927. Coffee, breakfast and lunch were on offer.

There are built-in wall benches and plain wooden tables. There are some extra seats in the sun lounge and tables and benches outside when the weather permits. There is also a children's play area.

It is a Thwaites house but the beers, including the very good bitter, are on handpump.

The Game Cock offers an extensive range of bar food at lunch-time and in the evening.

Opening times: Monday to Friday, 11.00 to 15.30 and 18.30 to 23.00; Saturday, 11.00 to 17.00 and 18.30 to 23.00; Sunday, 12.00 to 15.00 and 19.00 to 22.30.

THE WALK

Coming out of the Game Cock turn left, proceeding along the road to pass the village school before making another left turn, this time into Townhead Lane. Beyond the houses ignore the first stile on the left, signed to Clapham, and continue climbing to the crest of the first rise.

There make yet another left turn into Thwaite Lane, a bridleway also heading to Clapham. Within a few yards, however, take the ladder stile on the right which has a finger post alongside pointing to Norber.

Robin Proctor's Scar and Norber, near Austwick

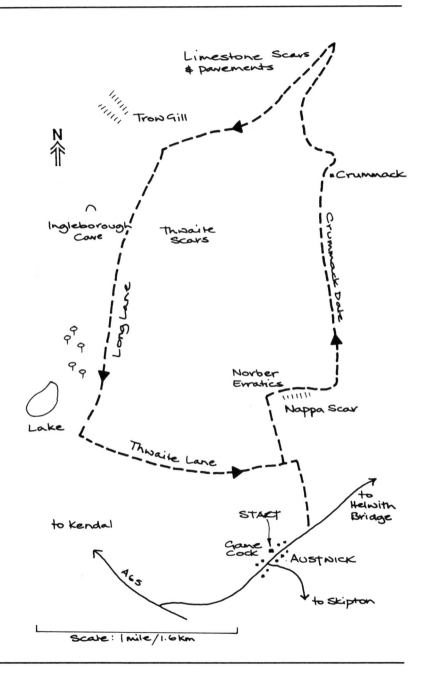

Staying a little to the right of a rough farm track, aim across the pastures towards a wall corner with Nappa Scar obvious a short distance away to the right.

There is a small gate in the corner. As it is chained, use the stone step stile a few yards to the right and, still keeping the wall on the left, climb towards the Norber erratics. These are a collection of slate boulders standing on limestone pedestals which were left high and dry by retreating ice.

Some 200 yards after the stile there is a junction of paths by a large slab of stone. Make an acute turn to the right, climbing a short distance to a footpath sign. Take the path pointing towards Crummack, first dropping through the boulders. On reaching a facing wall turn left to climb more steeply before negotiating a ladder stile on the right.

Over this proceed forward towards some trees and a wall gap. From there the path runs along a ledge on Nappa Scar and then to the right of a wall to another ladder stile affording access to Crummack Lane.

Turn left along this, ignoring any side paths and staying with it for well over a mile. It soon loses the metalled surface, at the same time offering a panorama of the Craven countryside. As it penetrates deeper in Crummack Dale it becomes lined on either side with a succession of limestone scars.

Where the lane swings sharply right towards a metal gate on its approach to Crummack Farm, stay forward, as signed, to walk to the left of a wall. Within 40 yards there is a five-barred gate followed, within 20 yards, by a second. On the far side of this maintain direction briefly, aiming for a ladder stile in the wall ahead.

However, do not proceed as far as this. Instead, at an obvious footpath junction take the left-hand track which is signed to Sulber.

A second junction is encountered where the gradient eases. Fork right to climb even higher into some splendid limestone country with Pen-y-ghent soon appearing away in the distance towards the right. On gaining the crest, Ingleborough shows itself directly ahead. This is the obvious point to pause and admire the all-round views along with a cup of coffee.

By the first stone cairn turn left along another broad grassy track which quickly veers round to the right as it heads for Long Scar before losing height slowly to a ladder stile. Centuries ago this was a packhorse route from Clapham to Askrigg.

After the ladder stile remain with the clear path as it moves diagonally left to a five-barred gate. Through this turn left, heading for a second gate.

From that point onwards the path develops into a stoney track which descends steeply for 100 yards before levelling-out to run between stone walls, the one on the right being partially derelict. In time there is a good view of the entrance to Trow Gill followed, soon afterwards, by Ingleborough Cave (See Ingleborough walk).

Continue along Long Lane, as it is known, for a further mile, passing to the left of 20 acres plantation before reaching a T-junction.

Turn left into Thwaite Lane for a further easy mile of pleasant walking until it forms a junction with Crummack Lane near Town Head, Austwick. Turn right to retrace the outward route to the Game Cock.

29. INGLETON FALLS

A walk through woodland glens where a series of waterfalls cascade over stone slabs to create scenes of almost magical beauty. The central section is over open limestone country with long distance views of the formidable bulk of Ingleborough.

Route: Ingleton – Swilla Glen – Pecca Falls – Thornton Force – Twistelton Hall – Beezley Falls – Snow Falls – Ingleton.

Distance: 4$^1/_4$ miles.

Start: The Craven Heifer, Ingleton. Map reference 694732

Map: Ordnance Survey Outdoor Leisure Map number 2, "Yorkshire Dales Western Area".

Public Transport: Bus service number 580, Skipton – Ingleton. Daily including Sundays. Pennine Bus Company.

Bus service numbers 279, 280, 281, Lancaster-Ingleton-Settle. Daily except Sundays. Ribble Bus Company and Lancaster City Transport.

Bus service number 279, 125 and 127, Kirkby Lonsdale – Ingleton. Daily except Sundays. Lancaster City Transport.

Bus service X98, Leeds-Grasmere. Summer Sundays only. Keighley and District Bus Company.

Dalesbus service number 809, Keighley – Skipton – Hawes – Settle. Tuesdays in late July and August only. Keighley and District Bus Company.

Dalesbus service number 800, Leeds – Grassington – Hawes – Ingleton. Summer Sundays and Bank holidays only. Keighley and District Bus Company.

Car: Ingleton is signed from the A65, Kendal – Skipton trunk road. There is a large car adjacent to the Community Centre in the middle of Ingleton village.

The Craven Heifer

Never mind the beer, order Yorkshire Pudding filled with steak and kidney. This is one of the many delicious bar meals served-up by John and Gina Sheehan, who are certain to accord any walker —or potholer or anyone else who cares to drop in — a very friendly welcome.

They serve Thwaite's Bitter, Brown and Pale along with a selection of bottled ales.

The bar, which is quite large, is subdivided into two sections and, like so many pubs in the Dales, has a beamed ceiling.

Opening Hours: Mondays to Fridays: 12.00 to 15.00 and 18.00 to 23.00. Saturdays: 11.30 to 15.00 and 18.00 to 23.00. Sundays: 12.00 to 15.00 and 19.00 to 10.30.

INGLETON

It is almost impossible to believe nowadays but Ingleton once boasted a colliery employing more than 300 miners. It was a hard life wresting coal from thin seams but the end came just a little over 50 years ago following a long and bitter struggle between the colliers and the mine owners. All the shafts have been filled-in and capped. The spoil heaps were levelled and grassed-over to create caravan sites.

The large viaduct remains as a reminder that Ingleton was once linked by rail with both Settle and Sedbergh. It was thanks to this once vital link that this village of narrow streets first became a tourist centre.

It is now recognised as one of the main starting points for an ascent of Ingleborough and offers dozens of other walking routes over the adjacent limestone countryside. It is also a popular centre for caving.

THE WALK

This is one of the most popular walks in the Dales so I debated about including it in this selection. In the end I came down in favour simply because it is such an attractive circuit and one which most people should have no problems with.

To visit Ingleton without completing the waterfalls walk is rather like eating a ham sandwich without mustard. I have few qualms on erosion grounds because a small fee is charged by the private owners and in general, the paths are well maintained.

Twistleton Scar, Ingleton

From the Craven Heifer, walk along Main Street towards the village centre. By the Three Horseshoes fork left down The Rake. At the bottom of the hill make another left turn into Bell Horse.

Still following the road, cross two stone bridges in quick succession, the first over the River Doe, the second over the River Twiss. A few yards after the end of the second turn right into Ingleton Falls car park.

Hand over your money at the kiosk before continuing forward with the Twiss on the right to enter a deciduous woodland. After the second gate enter Swilla Glen, a narrow, pretty limestone gorge. Cross to the far bank by turning right over Manor Bridge and then left along the path which clings to the right bank of the river.

Some distance upstream return to the left bank by crossing Pecca Bridge which gives an excellent view of the Pecca Falls as they

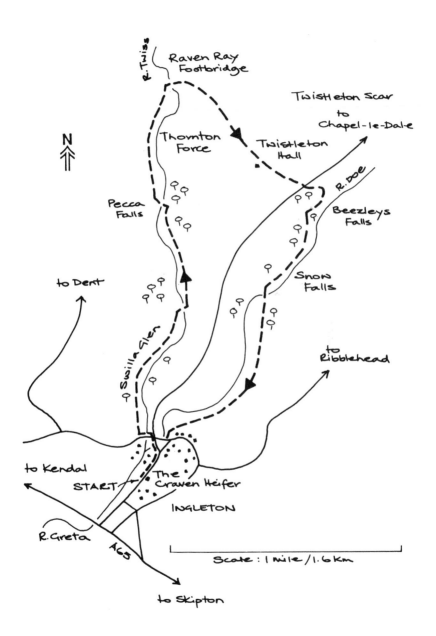

thunder over the limestone rocks. At this point, too, there is an opportunity to make a close inspection of the North Craven Fault, a geological feature created by movements in the earth's crust.

Climb the stepped path to the left of the falls. The more exposed and dangerous sections are protected by railings. By the top of the steps the trees are left behind and the valley opens out to reveal a different landscape. Stay with the path as it meanders over the limestone plateau to reach Thornton Force, one of the most impressive falls in the series.

Once again there are more steps to be climbed before the path levels to drop slightly towards Ravenray Footbridge after which there is a short climb to a gate. Once through this turn right into a walled lane which contours the hillside just below Twistleton Scar End.

After a kissing-gate followed by one of the five-barred variety there is an unusual prospect of Ingleborough looking from this angle like a formidable fortress.

Stay to the left of Twistelton Hall, now a working farm, to a step stile followed by a broad, grassy track which runs to the left of a wall in the direction of White Scar Cave. This is very prominent a little distance ahead and so, too, is the enormous quarry on the right.

White Scar, which is a public show cave, is one of the few which can accommodate wheelchairs. It has a marvellous and cleverly illumina-ted collection of stalagmites, stalactites and other rock formations. A visit requires a short deviation from this route.

The grass track heads down across an upland meadow to reach a gate in the wall flanking Oddies Lane, a former Roman road which is now metalled to link Ingleton with Chapel-le-Dale.

Cross directly into another surfaced lane which is signed as a footpath to Skirwith. In about 100 yards this corners to the right as it rounds Beezley farm. It then passes through a gate to become an unsurfaced bridleway.

Continue for 30 yards. There at a Y-junction, fork left onto a narrow path which, as it re-enters the woodland, becomes stepped.

It quickly leads down into a narrow, dramatic ravine where the River Doe tumbles over the Beezley Falls.

Remain with the path as it heads downstream passing the pretty Snow Falls and the North Craven Fault on the way. It crosses the river by means of a footbridge before gradually climbing away to run to the right of a new plantation and then into more open country.

On the outskirts of Ingleton it becomes Thacking Lane. At the first junction fork left to reach High Street by the Square and opposite the Post Office.

Turn right along High Street which, in turn, becomes Main Street as it leads back to the Craven Heifer.

30. INGLEBOROUGH

A walk to the summit of Ingleborough using one of the less well-trodden routes but returning by way of Gaping Gill and Trow Gill.

Route: Clapham − Newby − Little Ingleborough − Ingleborough summit − Gaping Gill − Trow Gill − Clapham.

Distance: $8^1/_2$ miles

Start: New Inn, Clapham. Map reference, 745691

Map: Ordnance Survey Outdoor Leisure Map number 2, "Yorkshire Dales, Western Area."

Public transport: Clapham is served by several trains daily on the Leeds-Lancaster line. NOTE: Clapham station is approximately $1^1/_2$ miles from the village centre.

Bus service 580, Skipton − Ingleton. Daily, including Sundays. Pennine Bus Company.

Bus service 279, Settle − Lancaster. Daily except Sundays. Lancaster City Transport.

Dalesbus service number 809, Keighley-Skipton-Settle-Hawes. Tuesdays only in late July and August. Keighley and District Bus Company.

Car: Clapham is signposted from the A65 road between Ingleton and Settle. There is a Yorkshire Dales National Park car park and Information Centre about 100 yards from the New Inn.

THE NEW INN, CLAPHAM

Hosts Keith and Barbara Mannion are keen hill-walkers themselves and so not only provide a warm welcome for ramblers but even provide a drying room.

It is recommended by Les Routiers and, in April 1991, was presented with the Pub of the Year Award by Country Walking magazine. A former coaching inn overlooking Clapham Beck, the bar is cosy and beamed. In addition to a selection of bar meals it also boasts a restaurant with an extensive a la carte menu. It has 13 bedrooms all with en-suite facilities.

It serves Dent Bitter, Tetley's Bitter, Younger's number 3, McEwan's 80 Shilling plus a guest beer which changes regularly.

Opening times: Monday to Saturday, 11.30 to 15.30 and 19.00 to 23.00; Sundays, 12.00 to 15.00 and 19.00 to 22.30. In summer it tends to remain open all day.

CLAPHAM

With old stone houses lining either side of the beck, Clapham forms a picturesque village. It owes its importance to its position on the former Kendal-Skipton turnpike and, in more recent times, as a starting point for many of the routes up Ingleborough.

Most of the buildings date from the 1760s when the Farrar family became owners of the estate.

Clapham Beck

INGLEBOROUGH

One of the famous Three Peaks of the Yorkshire Dales. The summit is a large, flat plateau with not only a triangulation pillar at 723 metres, also a stone-built wind shelter in the form of a cross with a view-finder set into the centre. The panorama is extensive, stretching out over large sections of limestone pavement to include the tops of Whernside and Pen-y-ghent.

The most spectacular sight, however, and one every rambler aspires to enjoy, is the Ribblehead Viaduct away to the north. Its 24 graceful arches enable the Settle-Carlisle Railway to cross one of the bleakest and dourest stretches of moorland in the country.

Opened in 1875, after five years of construction work, it cost the lives of many navvies who now lie buried in the serenity of the churchyard at Chapel-le-Dale.

Along the eastern side of the plateau are the remains of several prehistoric hut circles and a stone wall, the latter allegedly built by the Romans as part of a signalling station but, arguably erected by a local tribe of Celts as a defence against the Romans.

GAPING GILL

One of the largest pot-holes in the country. On certain Bank Holiday week-ends, courtesy of the local caving club, it is possible to sit in a bosun's chair for the descent through a narrow chimney into an enormous chamber some 360 feet high. It is large enough to accommodate York Minster.

TROW GILL

A narrow rocky defile. A skeleton, claimed by some to be that of a German spy, was discovered there in 1947.

INGLEBOROUGH CAVE

This show cave was opened-up in 1837 when a limestone wall, impounding a large underground lake, was demolished by explosives. The cave is linked to Gaping Gill.

CLAPDALE WOODS

The route through these follows the Reginald Farrar nature trail. He was a local botanist in the early part of the nineteenth century who travelled widely in the Alps, Himalayas, Japan and Burma. He amassed a varied collection of exotic plant species which are planted in the woodlands.

Spring is a good time to pay a visit when the floor is carpeted with blue bell, wood anemone, primrose and wild garlic. There is an admission charge (currently 15 pence) payable at the cottage at the Clapham end of the trail.

THE WALK

From the New Inn cross the road bridge spanning Clapham Beck and, at the junction stay forward to pass the Post Office on the left. Within a few yards turn right into Haw Lane, continuing beyond the traffic de-restriction signs for approximately a quarter of a mile.

Turn left into a signed bridleway. This is Laithbutts Lane which, in parts, is overgrown with nettles. Initially it is walled on both sides but, after the first five-barred gate, crosses a meadow a little to the left of a hedge.

Maintain direction beyond the next gate to a third, which is waymarked, and a fourth. Beyond that the track reverts to a walled lane as it goes to the right of Laithbutts Farm. 15 yards beyond a stile it emerges onto a minor road on the outskirts of the hamlet of Newby.

Turn right along this road for half a mile to reach the Old Road linking Clapham with Ingleton. Cross directly onto a broad track which keeps to the left of Newby Cote, a farm with an impressive house of mellow stone, to enter a walled lane.

Beyond a ladder stile veer slightly left, away from a more obvious track, to walk alongside a wall. Where this ends go slightly to the left, following a vague path over open moorland to pass in front of two sets of grouse butts.

After passing a swallow hole, aim directly for the cairned summit of Little Ingleborough which, in fine weather, is clearly visible. This approach involves more gradual climbing than most other routes.

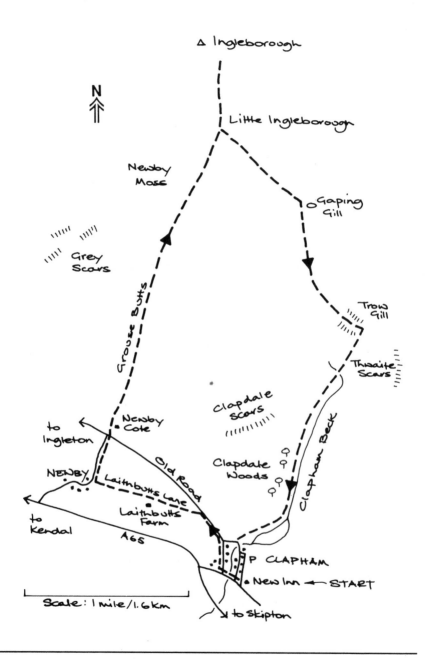

From Little Ingleborough continue forward along the broad path, sections of which have recently been re-surfaced as part of the Three Peaks Project undertaken by the National Park as part of its anti-erosion campaign.

Ingleborough carries a sting in its tail. The final pitch tracks diagonally up the hillside before emerging onto the summit plateau.

From the summit retrace your steps to Little Ingleborough but turn left by the cairns to embark on a steep, rocky descent. This levels out before reaching the fenced-off enclosure surrounding the entrance to Gaping Gill.

By the pot-hole turn right onto a broad track which soon swings left across level ground to a tall ladder stile. Immediately over that, fork right to another ladder stile and the entrance to the sombre, rocky defile of Trow Gill where caution is needed if recent rain has made the stones slippery.

As the lower end of the gill is reached Thwaite Scars come into view directly ahead but the path, now widened into a track, turns right before crossing an old stone packhorse bridge to pass the entrance to Ingleborough Cave.

Continue along the track, known at this point as Clapdale Road, to enter Clapdale Woods.Ramblers wishing to avoid paying the 15 pence charge for using the nature trail should veer right up the slope to regain Clapham by way of Clapdale Farm and the road. After passing a small lake on the left, the main train track reaches a metalled road. Turn left along this and then right into Riverside to walk alongside Clapham Beck to the New Inn.

Sample the delights of country pubs, and enjoy some of the finest walks with our expanding range of 'real ale' books:

PUB WALKS IN THE PEAK DISTRICT – Les Lumsdon and Martin Smith

***MORE* PUB WALKS IN THE PEAK DISTRICT
– Les Lumsdon and Martin Smith**

PUB WALKS IN THE PENNINES – Les Lumsdon and Colin Speakman

PUB WALKS IN LANCASHIRE – Neil Coates

PUB WALKS IN THE LAKE DISTRICT – Neil Coates

PUB WALKS IN THE COTSWOLDS – Laurence Main

**HEREFORDSHIRE WALKS – REAL ALE AND CIDER COUNTRY
– Les Lumsdon**

PUB WALKS IN CHESHIRE – Jen Darling

There are even more books for outdoor people in our catalogue, including:

EAST CHESHIRE WALKS – Graham Beech

WEST CHESHIRE WALKS – Jen Darling

WEST PENNINE WALKS – Mike Cresswell

NEWARK AND SHERWOOD RAMBLES – Malcolm McKenzie

RAMBLES AROUND MANCHESTER – Mike Cresswell

WESTERN LAKELAND RAMBLES – Gordon Brown

WELSH WALKS: Dolgellau and the Cambrian Coast – Laurence Main

OFF-BEAT CYCLING IN THE PEAK DISTRICT – Clive Smith

THE GREATER MANCHESTER BOUNDARY WALK – Graham Phythian

And there's more . . .

**Guidebooks for local towns; A guide to the pubs of 'Old Lancashire';
Spooky stories; Myths and Legends; Football books
and, under our Sigma Press banner,
over 100 computer books!**

All of our books are available from your local bookshop.
In case of difficulty, or to obtain our complete catalogue, please contact:

**Sigma Leisure,
1 South Oak Lane,
Wilmslow, Cheshire SK9 6AR**

Phone: 0625 - 531035 Fax: 0625 - 536800; ACCESS and VISA welcome!